E-Content in Teaching

ABOUT THE BOOK

The present century is rightly called the technological century. The development in various aspects of computer technology has reached beyond our imagination and expectations. Science and technology play a significant role in the formation of modern civilization in any society. The increasing scientific and technological impact upon human life activities is developing the scientific attitude of people. Computer Assisted Instruction (CAI) has emerged as an effective and efficient media of instruction in the advanced countries of the world. CAI is being used in the formal and non-formal educations at all levels. In India too computer has been introduced in most of the areas such as data processing, decision making, etc., it has impact on the working methods of research and development in the field of Science and Technology

ABOUT AUTHOR

Dr. R.Annadurai is working as Director-in-Charge in Centre for Educational Research at Madurai Kamaraj University in Madurai, Tamil Nadu. He was served Fourteen years in College of Education and University, Experience in field of Education. He is Editor in Chief for International Journal of Educational Research, Development and Extension (IJERDE) at Centre for Educational Research-MKU- He has served as member in the visiting team conducted by NCTE, Bangalore. He was presented the research papers in many National and International conferences and organizing many Conference, Seminar and Workshop related to academic Activities.

E-Content in Teaching

Dr. R.Annadurai

Director-in-Charge in Centre for Educational Research
Madurai Kamaraj University
Madurai, Tamil Nadu

AMIGA PRESS INC.
DELHI (INDIA)

AMIGA PRESS INC.
Registered Office:
19 DBS Building, Ansari Road, Darya Ganj, Delhi. 110002, India
Phone: +91-11-23283333 Email: amigapress@gmail.com

This edition is published by Amiga Press Inc.

ISBN: 978-93-84533-56-4

First Published 2020

Reprint 2024

Printed and bound in India by Replika Press Pvt. Ltd.

Contents

1.

Comparative Study of Effectiveness of Computer Assisted Instruction on Circulatory System for IX Standard Students

INTRODUCTION

This study investigated the compare effectiveness of computer-assisted instruction (CAI) and conventional teaching method in biology on senior high school students. A science class was selected in each of two randomly selected schools. The pre-test, post-test equivalent quasi experimental design was used. The students in the experimental group learned science concepts (circulatory system) through the CAI, whereas the students in the control group were taught the same concepts by the conventional approach. The conventional approach consisted of teaching, discussions and question and answer teaching methods. The students' pre-test and post-tests scores were subjected to Analysis of't' Test, ANOVA. The results indicated that students that were instructed by the experimental group performed better on the post-test than those instructed by the conventional approach. This may help teachers in organizing meaningful teaching learning experiences and adopt innovative methods and approaches in teaching. Computer assisted Instruction (CAI) is a supplementary instructional strategy ineffective teaching. In this paper, researcher elaborates use, utility and importance of CAI in teaching-Learning. To create new approaches technique and appropriate digital learning environment applying in education for present and future generation. Based on the research findings recommendations were made on the need to develop relevant

CAI packages for teaching-Learning biology in secondary schools.

Education should be an individual activity to a much greater content. Not at all children should be forced to go through the same steps of learning at the same speed. The high achievers will move faster in their learning where as the under achievers will need more time. Children have their own ways of learning. Some children may learn better through the use of different learning materials them by merely listening to an inspirational talk by the teacher. The style of learning may also change according to age. They use their season in acquiring knowledge. An important feature of education is its use of physical and intellectual tools. Education must reflect the influence of technology. This new technology demands new interpretations of the instructional process and those changed with educating the next generation must engage in a continual cycle of education and revaluation in the light of technological influence at all levels.

EDUCATION TECHNOLOGY

Educational technology is not a simple combination of these two words. It is usually thought of even more than the sum of the following two interpretations.

1. Technology in Educatione the effectiveness of the educatioal l combination or seperately bjective - vis-a
2. Technology of Education

TECHNOLOGY IN EDUCATION

This is based on the application of engineering principle for developing electro mechanical equipment like motion pictures, tape – recorders, teaching machines, computers, television etc. This approach of education a technology is a bye product of the 21th century. **DAVIS** (1971) thinks that the hardware approach is based on the application of physical science to the education and training system which mechanics the process of teaching gradually so that teachers would be able to deal with more students resulting in less cost and economy in finances. It is said that good teachers have always used visual ads to assist their teaching ancient great masters used illustrations and models to increase the interests of their students. Today educational technology is stressing modern audio – visual and computer equipment.

TECHNOLOGY OF EDUCATION

It refers to the study of principles and theories, formulate to solve problems in the teaching, learning process. The main frame work of education technology is provided by Technology or Education. 'Technology in Education' provides the support to implement the broader instructional design. It primarily implies systematic approach to instructional design incorporating alternative methodologies, media and aids with reference to the objective vis-à-vis learning content. This accommodates the systems approach, programmed learning etc.

According to the **encyclopedia of education** (1971. vol-9 P.22) Educational

Technology is the purposeful combination or separately of objects, techniques, devices, events and relationships to increase the effectiveness of the educational process.

APPLICATION OF EDUCATION TECHNOLOGY

Educational Technology has gradually influenced and developed the teaching learning process. Since the world is moving towards Technological growth information and special place in education. The trend is to introduce technological principles in the classroom. Educational technology consists of all modern media, methods and materials, which can be used to maximizing the learning experience of student at various levels.

HISTORICAL PERSPECTIVE OF INDIVIDUAL INSTRUCTION

The classical conditioning of **PAVLOV** opened a new chapter in teaching and learning and the behaviour gave importance to reinforcement as a major condition for learning. Edward Thorn dike improved the reinforcement procedure with stimulus (reinforce) response reaction, **SKINNER** (1967) expanded this idea as operative conditioning which led to the invention of teaching machine. Both kin aesthetic and information feedback are identified to play crucial role in skill learning by **GAGNE** (1963) **LUMSDANOE** (1964) proposed a new definition to instructional technique which was later applied in programmed instruction. The five golden rules applied in this preparation of programmed learning material (PLM) and the need for defining the objectives in behavioural terms in the preparation of instructional software material are proposed as essential by **DANIEL DAVIS** (1965). The three phases that help the teacher to decide in the ongoing focus on pedagogy are; what to teach (objectives) whom to teach (entering behaviour) and how to flash the procedures which are similar to the CAI model. **FLANDERS'** (1964) recommendation for interactivity in learning are subjoined through various learning activities built in the CAI package.

INDIVIDUALISED INSTRUCTION

Individualized instruction is the one-to-one relationship between a student and what he learns (**DUNN** and **DUNN** 1977). Individualized instruction is one of the most active areas in the education innovations. This kind of instruction helps the learner to learn at his own pace. Modern class rooms are characterized by a high degree of heterogeneity. Individual differences are pronounced among learners in large classes and to cater to the needs of the learners in such classes individualized instruction bodies is required.

Through individualized instruction materials self learning can be enhanced. This land of self learning helps the learners to learn even more difficult contents and learning of higher categories. Through self learning the needs and levels of the learners are considerably satisfied. The individual differences are considered and hence individualized instruction certainly leads to mastery level of learning.

Individualized instruction may be provided for the following reasons (**DUNN** and **DUNN** 1977)

1. A gifted student, able to come with new consents or skills independently may work well ahead of his peers through the use of this method. He need not wait to learn until the teacher can work with him individually or the rest of his peers catch up with him.
2. An interested student may learn more about a given topic, consent or skill after most of his peers have mastered it, may spend as much time as needed reinforcing the knowledge at his desire and pace until he too is ready to move ahead.
3. An interested student may learn more about a given topic, consents or skill at the moment in time when he wants to, not when the teacher is able to get to the subject.
4. An average student who cares to something new in an interesting way may become sufficiently motivated to work on his own because of the nature of the varied multi sensory experience.

Individualized instruction materials should have certain characteristics. According to **MORE** (1968), an individualized instructional material should have the following features. It should as

1. Permit the learners to explore freely.
2. Inform the learner about the consequence of his action.
3. Be self – pacing that is the student can more at his own rate of learning.
4. Permit the learner to make full use of his capacity for discovering relations of various kinds.

GOLDSCHMID (1973) maintain that any form of individualized instruction should possess the following characters. It should

1. Emphasize learning
2. Ensure active students participation
3. Stress evaluation and feed back
4. Principle of individual pacing

There are different forms of individualized instruction. Some of them are

1. Learning Module
2. Multimedia Package
3. Programmed Learning Material (PLM)
4. Personalized system of instruction (PSI)
5. Audio Tutorial Instruction (ATI)

LEARNING MODULE

A learning module is a short unit of instruction dealing with a single unit of subject matter self contained with define objectives. Based on the specified instructional objectives, questions are given and the learner assesses his/her performance in the subject.

Multimedia Package

A multimedia package consists of a collection of soft ware's of several media dealing with a specific topic on subject area and forming an integrated whole. Based on the interest and aptitude of the students, the students can select the media through which they want to learn the subject.

Programmed Learning Material (PLM)

Skinner has pronounced Programmed Learning Material (PLM) based on the theory of operant conditioning PLM consists of planned sequence of learning activity for achieving mastery in terms of stimulus response reinforcement relationship.

Personalized System of Instruction (PSI)

The Personalized System of Instruction refers to training which is based on self pacing and master learning. In PSI, learners work in their own and they must achieve mastery of a series of written learning unit. They are assisted by teachers and professors. It is possible to apply PSI.

Audio Tutorial Instruction (ATI)

Here the instructor's remarks, directions and interpretations of learning assignments and resources are given through audio cassettes. The cassettes are prepared by the concerned subject experts keeping in mind the target for which the cassette is prepared. Even for distance education system, audio cassettes are being used for instruction.

COMPUTER ASSISTED INSTRUCTION (CAI)

The most exciting innovation in educational technology is the Computer Assisted Instruction (CAI). Though it was not skill developed like other individualized instructional materials, the day is not far off when it will revolutionize the whole process of instruction. **TANEJA (1999)**

A computer is programmed with linear or branching programmes. It acts like a super teaching machine catering to the needs of a number of students at the same time. The characteristic aspects of the CAI is its capacity to initiate flexible instructional with the student. In this respect it is superior to the teaching machine. The computer can do this in different ways. The computer is able to record and store all the responses of all the students. It can use the information in deciding what information is to be given to the student next. It can branch not just in terms of on answer but also in terms of a whole series of previous answers. It can also record the time taken to answer a question and the decree of correctness of the student's response. It uses the information in planning to determine which branch or format would be conductive to a learner for effective instruction.

Computer Assisted Instruction is not merely a sophisticated type of programmed instruction but a different kind of instruction but a different kind of instruction altogether. No doubt, data processing, data communication, consents of audio-visual and media theory, communication theory, system theory and learning theory are annelid in the preparation of the CAI material. In contrast to CAI, Computer Managed Instruction (CMI) analysis the relationship between various factors concerned with the learning of a pupil and suggests activities appropriate to individual students.

DIFFERENT FORMS OF COMPUTER ASSISTED INSTRUCTION

Computer Assisted Instruction can be take any one of the following modes depending on the purpose of the material, the five different modes of CAI are

(a) Drill and Practice
(b) Tutorial Mode
(c) Simulation Mode
(d) Discovery Mode
(e) Gaming Mode

Tutorial Mode

In this mode information is presented in small units followed by a question. The student's response is analyzed by the computer and an appropriate feedback is provided. This is similar to programmed instruction. As in programmed instruction, the information may be given in a linear fashion as in branched pathways. The greater the number of alternative paths, more adaptive the tutorial can be to individuals.

Drill and Practice Mode

The learner, provided with a number of graded examples on the concepts and principles learnt earlier. The idea is to develop proficiency and fluency through doing all the correct responses are reinforced and the incorrect responses are diagnosed and corrected. The compute continues the drill and the learners continue his practice until mastery is achieved by the learner.

Simulation Mode

In this mode, the learners are presented with scheduled down stimulated. Situations bearing correspondence with real situation. Simulations are made to avoid risk, save money and conserve time, simulation of an aero plane in flight, an experiment on titration, a nuclear reaction, collision of two bodies are good examples of the simulation models in science.

Discovery Mode

The individual approach to teaching and learning is as followed. The learner is encouraged to proceed through trial and error approach i.e., by solving a given problem, realizing where and how he/she went wrong, trying again and finally solving the complex problem.

Gaming Mode

In this mode, the learner is engaged in playing opposite. The computer or opposite another learner. The extent of learning depends upon the type of the game. Games on spelling names of places and general knowledge are some examples of the gaming mode.

Information Handling

One area where processing and information handling capacity of computer is profitably used in counseling and guiding the computer stores complete cumulative records and match them against employment needs and potentialities as required for personal and vocational guidance.

MERITS OF COMPUTER ASSISTED INSTRUCTION

Computer Assisted Instruction has several advantages over other systems of instructions.

1. Each student receives instruction at his own pace
2. Each student receives immediate feedback for his response
3. Each student responds continuously as he receives instruction
4. All units of learning are broke down into subunits and elements of learning in accordance with skinner's approach of teaching in small steps
5. Reinforcement of learning is achieved by personal message
6. Learning sessions are not manageable by designing the duration between half an hour to one hour
7. Student can access the computer any place
8. Students can learn in their own styles and ways
9. Students can test their own learning at any point of time to an end
10. Lesson from the theories of learning are taken into account at stage instructional design
11. Teacher's time is saved from the routine job of giving activity and employed in innovative instruction design and student guidance

OBJECTIVES OF THE STUDY

1. To understand about computer system and its working
2. To understand the educational application of computer
3. To develop scientific attitude among school students
4. To provide a broad – based biological knowledge, stimulate a deep interest in the natural world
5. To develop a CAI package for self instruction on the unit circulatory system in science for IX standard students
6. To enable the pupils to utilize effectively the instructional material in learning biology

7. To verify whether there is any difference in learning level between
    a) Boys and Girls
    b) Rural and Urban School
    c) Government, Government Aided and Unaided Schools

HYPOTHESIS

1. There is no significant difference between the pretest and posttest scores of government school pupils' following the Computer Assisted Instruction.
2. There is no significant difference between the pretest and posttest scores of Aided School Pupils' following the Computer Assisted Instruction.
3. There is no significant difference between the pretest and posttest scores of Unaided School Pupil following the Computer Assisted Instruction.
4. There is no significant difference between the pretest and posttest mean scores of the experimental group following Computer Assisted Instruction.
5. There is no significant difference in post test performance of Computer Assisted Instruction between the different types of school pupil.
6. There is no significant difference between the post test performance of Urban and Rural school pupil following Computer Assisted Instruction.
7. There is no significant difference between the post test performance of Boys and Girls following Computer Assisted Instruction.

SCOPE OF THE STUDY

1. The students can get more and adequate knowledge through self instruction material.
2. It helps the students to develop self study habits, since individual study can be brought out with the help of self instruction material.
3. The study is expected to help the students at all levels, since computer plays a vital role in all the aspects of life especially in the field of education.
4. The present study is experimental study to compose the effectiveness of CAI and on "Circulatory System" for IX standard students.
5. In future instruction materials will act as a source of the knowledge for the teacher and students.
6. It will help the teacher in the teaching learning process, as it can draw the attention of the students by teaching learning computer.

STUDIES CONDUCTED ON CAI IN INDIA

In India at present several efforts are being taken up to develop the software for CAI, for individual instruction several studies also have been conducted to identify the effectiveness of CAI and Handout over the achievement of the students. SHARMA and GEORGE (1979) developed a CAI package of mathematics. Their objectives were to study the effectiveness of the CAI for school children and the findings revealed that the CAI packages produced significant result over the achievement of the children. BADRINATH (1986) conducted a study on developing and validating CAI package for reflection of light at the VIII standard level. He found that experience in CAI program appeared to be an effective method than the conventional method.

NACHIMUTHU (1988) has studied the development of CAI program on "Leaves". He expressed in his thesis about the difficulties in programming a lesson. He also suggested that teaching will be more effective if the researcher himself programmed the lesson than using readymade diskettes. Because when the research programme, he can give all the points to be taught, as in conventional method and so the learners also will score marks up to the researchers' expectation.

PALANIAPPAN (1989) made a study on computers in education. He found that after introducing computers is schools for teaching, the attitude of teachers as well as students have changed. Many dull students scoreless through CAI, than the conventional method.

HEMALATHA (1989) studied on orientation of CAI. She concluded that the computers are commonly used in three main response sensitive strategies in CAI and suggested some levels of comparative involvement in decision making feature. They are drill and practice, tutorial and dialogue.

KARPAGA KUMARAVEL. R (1990) in his study on the effectiveness of computer assisted instruction video assisted instruction and conventional instruction in English language learning found that the achievement of video assisted instruction group in better than computer assisted instruction and conventional instructional group.

P. JEYAMANI (1991) pointed out that learning with computers offers a very powerful tool for educators and all efforts must be made to learners the potential of computers in education. This educational technology could therefore have a more on comparing role to play in the developing world. Thus the stimulation model of teaching through computer assisted instruction can readily be used for all types of teaching.

SARVANAN. M (1991) developed and validated a CAI package on X – rays for XI standard students. His findings revealed that the CAI packages were effective for individualized instruction.

PURUSHOTHAMAN and STELLA (1991) studied the effectiveness of CAI learning testing and guidance. The study reported that for low achievers self-testing and guidance through computer was found to be more effective.

BENEDICTO (1992) developed and validated a CAI packages on pollution for XI standard Biology students. The major findings of his study was learning the unit through CAI was faster for both slow and fast learners when compared with traditional teaching. He also reported the software developed ensures uniformity of achievement among Biology students.

MATHIVANAN (1994) attempted to develop and validate a CAI package on organisms an environment for IX standard pupils. His report revealed that the CAI package produced more significant effect on the achievement of the pupils of knowledge, comprehension, application and analysis level.

Dr.P.ANNARAJA and Smt. NIRMALA SUNDARARAJ (2005) made a study on power point presentation in teaching zoology pre post design was used in this that, they found that the power point presentation is effective in teaching zoology for higher secondary students.

JAYAKRUSHA CHOUDHARY (2005) conducted a study on effect of Computer Assisted Learning using method of enquiry in teaching physics in secondary school. Main objectives of this study was to test the efficiency of computer aided learning using method of inquiry in teaching physics at the secondary level on achievement and concept attainment. He found that CAI experimental method is to be more effective than conventional method of teaching.

G.SUBRAMANIAN (2006) pointed out major findings were computer assisted instruction significantly improves the performance of students, learning accountancy at higher secondary level. The combination of the colour, text, music and animation of the CAI package was well received by the students and the positive effect of same is perceptible from their achievement scores.

A computer factorial program on the laws and consents encountered in introductory physics courses among high school students was studied by EAUGHN AND KUHN (1979) these programmer were written with the weaker students in mind. But the researchers found that even stronger students used them presumably to check whether or not they really understood a particular phenomenon. This success was attributed to the fact that the programs were written so that each student's incorrect answer was dealt with in the novelty of using the computer encouraged students usage much more than the prospect of working from a study guide.

In another study, the efforts of CAI and reinforcement schedules on physics achievement towards physics of high school were measured by BANNET (1986). Seventy one high school students were taken as sample. The result of this study supported that students who received CAI would achieve significantly higher physics test scores. .

PASCUAL (1993) conducted a twofold study. He applied linguistics approach and empirical study designed to measure the degree of motivation in students learning English using CAI material and Non CAI material. He found that students belonging to CAI material showed more motivation than their counterparts.

SIEGLE (2000) the purpose of this study was to investigate whether exposure to multimedia and presentation software on laptop computers influenced student achievement in a secondary level anatomy and physiology science course. The study demonstrated that students learned more when they had access to laptop computers, were exposed to multimedia software, and created projects with presentation software.

VENDLINSKI et al (2002) conducted a quasi-experimental study with 134 first-year high school chemistry students using the Interactive Multimedia

Exercises computer based learning and assessment tool to solve qualitative chemistry problems. Results of this study show a strong and significant correlation between computer aided measures of student understanding and the teacher's manual evaluation of student understanding using her own rubric.

SUSAN et al (2003) in his study examined 165 teachers' beliefs about student centered learning as they implemented Alien Rescue, a computer based programme for middle school science that was designed to create a Student Centered Learning Environment (SCLE) in the class room. Discusses the goal of student activity, the role of the teacher, assessment, and student interaction.

RABIA TABASSUM (2004) conducted a study on effect of Computer Assisted Instruction CAI on the Secondary School Students Achievement in Science. In his study analysis of data revealed that the class IX standard students taught through computer assisted instruction as supplementary strategy performed significantly better. The CAI was found equally effective for both male and female students.

WINTERS et al (2005) in this study 62 high school biology students, paired heterogeneously based on prior knowledge, learned about genetic using Gen Scope, a Computer Based Learning Environment. The results of this naturalistic study could potentially be used to inform educational practice by highlighting scaffolds that may foster self-regulated learning in a CBLE mediated science inquiry context.

HARSKAMP et al (2005) conducted a study on solving Physics Problems with the help of Computer Assisted Instruction" In this study the main goal of most Physics text books is to develop declarative and procedural knowledge exercises provide pupils with opportunities to apply this knowledge. The computer group taking part in the experiment did achieve higher results in solving problems.

CEPNI et al (2006) pointed out that the study on effects of Computer Assisted Instruction Material related to photosynthesis topic on student cognitive development misconceptions and attitudes. This study result showed that using CAIM in teaching photo synthesis topic was very effective for students to reach comprehension and application levels of cognitive domain.

MAHAMOOD FARHADIAN (2007) in his research, he studied the co-operative learning, Computer Assisted Instruction and combination of these two methods called Co-operative Computer Assisted Instruction (CCAI). In CCAI method with the use of computer and attractive software, there would be appropriate grounds in instruction and educational achievement of mathematics for students. This method was examined for small group of student in a workshop. He had investigated some hypotheses on reduce of the students negative beliefs about mathematics, the speed of learning mathematics and its independence from time scheduling. Findings of the study, the difference between pretest and posttest scores were meaningfully significant.

METHODOLOGY

Educational software development and validation is a major research and development activity in the field of education. The major area in educational software is occupied by the instructional software development. The nature and the impact of computer and learning were led to its acquiring more significance. In the latest concept of improvement in the instructional software produced and the role played by educational technologists in the consents and process of software development. The CAI package depends on the electronic device. Further there is need for the subject export, technical expert. Individualized instruction is the one-to-one relationship between learners and the subject to be learnt.

SELECTION OF AREA

The investigator has selected six schools in Udumalpet at Tiruppur District which come under the Tamil Nadu State Board of Education. The sample selected for study consists of boys and girls from rural and urban schools.

SELECTION OF THE SAMPLE

Sample selection is an important aspect of the research study, violation of a proper sampling method may yield based information of research and therefore maximum care is necessary for solution of sample.

English medium students of standard were selected from different types study the investigator selected three hundred students. Hundred and fifty boys and hundred and fifty girls of ninth standard from two government schools, two governments aided schools and two unaided schools have been selected.

Considering the non-feasibility of formulating randomized groups in a school setting, it was decided to have purposive sampling as the method of sampling for this experiment. Hundred and fifty students of Class IX in each of the three type of schools were taken as CAI experimental group and hundred and fifty students of

Hundred and fifty students of Class IX in different types of rural schools and hundred and fifty students of Class IX in different types of urban schools were taken as the experimental group. The same schools are brought under the categories, group of different variables are follow. Purposive sampling procedure is applied for selecting the sampling and so that it is free from any prejudice. The following table presents the details of the samples selected for the study.

SAMPLING TECHNIQUE

For the present study purposive sampling method is used. The purposive sampling is selected by some arbitrary method because it is known to be representative of the total population. It is appropriate in a study which lays special emphasis on the control of certain specific variables.

DESIGN OF THE STUDY

The design selected for the study is the pretest and posttest of two groups.

a. Administrating a pretest measuring the dependent variable at initial stage for elimination of novelty factor.
b. Applying the treatment to the subject, to measure treatment effect.
c. Administering a posttest again for measuring the impact of the dependent variable.

Differences attributed to application of the experimental treatment are then determined by comparing pretest and posttest scores.

DEVELOPMENT OF INSTRUCTIONAL MATERIALS

The subject is to be converted into CAI package was "Circulatory System" in biology for IX standard students. The content frame work of the syllabus was adapted from the prescribed text by the Tamil Nadu State Board Text Book for IX standard. The teaching points were collected from the text books and other reference books mentioned and sequence according to the designed learning level of students in the local school. The content prescribed was corrected into a reading material in simple language according to their vocabulary level.

The teaching frames were structured on the learning materials following the norms and theories set for the preparation of CAI package. The teaching points were structured in small dosage called "Frame". Frames were arranged in proper sequence. In each frame information was presented with simple illustration or examples.

Objectives Starting Phase

Bloom's Taxonomy was used for objective formation specific behavioral objective was formulated as performance objectives on completion of learning the unit "Circulatory System" the student should be able to identify. Content analysis was done. Care was taken to link the content by appropriate sequencing strategy.

1. Define "Blood"
2. State the composition of blood
3. Name the types of blood
4. List the properties of blood
5. Distinguish RBC, WBC and Platelet
6. Describe the functions of blood and
7. Define "Blood Group"

DESCRIPTION OF THE TOOL USED

a) Computer Assisted Instruction Package: The instructional soft ware package developed to help the learners through a prescribed form of self instruction the subject are to be converted into frame. In this study in biology CAI package was Circulatory System for IX standard students. This CAI package contains various stimuli such as showing pictures and animation. This CAI was an instructional effective material individualized.

b) Performa Sheet: The investigator herself has developed a Performa sheet to collect necessary information regarding the individuals back ground such as the name, age, sex, name and address of the school, locality, type of school, system of school,

c) Science Achievement Test: In this present study the investigator was prepared the achievement test question paper based on the IX standard State Board Syllabus. The question has been given to IX students of the selected school situated in and around Coimbatore. In consists of 40 questions and each objective has been provided 4 multiple choice from which the individual is asked to mark the response which he/she feels to be right in their point of view.

d) Scoring Key: The answer scripts for the conducted achievement test were collected and scored based on the scoring key. The score the test it was decided to give one mark as weight age for each correct answer. Thus a maximum of 40 marks who give correct response for all the items.

JURY OPINION

The copies of achievement test were submitted to a group of five subject experts who are teachers in schools and colleges for their valuable suggestion. Based on their ideas, the structure of questions was modified, options of some questions were changed and the number of question was also increased. They were asked to examine whether the items fully covered the content of "Circulating System" presented for IX standard by Tamil Nadu Text-book society. Items which were choose or similar or deviant was dropped as recommended by experts. They items reflected the entire context. Thus the context validity of the test was established based on expert judgments. As a result the test tool for the final study was prepared with forty multiple choice questions.

PILOT STUDY

Pilot study is a vital factor is any research. The pilot study administered to 50 student of IX standard level.

ADMINISTRATION OF TOOL

The study was conducted and materials were distributed to the students after taking prior permission from the head master of the selected schools. The investigator personally visited each school and collected the data. The purpose and intention of the study were briefly explained. The subjects had been repeatedly assured that they could freely express their opinions without and reservation since the purpose was purely educational research. The co-operation extended by the respondents/students was encouraging remarkable.

METHODS OF EXPERIMENTATION

Each sample was pre-tested with criteria referenced test to measure the entry level. Before the experiment or treatment the students were pre-tested using the test. The test was helpful in accessing subject knowledge of the students prior to treatment. The same test was administered again after treatment effects. The individual instruction analysis was carried by employing't' test for difference between the CAI groups.

DATA COLLECTION

As presented pre test, post test was planned to achieve the objective of the study. The sample was selected for conducting the experiment. For conducting the experiment the investigator selected six Higher Secondary School, The investigator selected Higher Secondary School hence it would be easy to provide the treatment in the school to the sample.

STATISTICAL TECHNIQUES USED IN THE STUDY

Appropriate statistical techniques were used which included the mean, standard deviation, t-test and ANOVA.

ANALYSIS AND INERPRETATION OF THE DATA

Computation of Statistics

The first section deals with background information of the selected sample based on age, gender, type of school, educational status of parents, and socio-economic status of the family. In second section the scores of pre test and post test were calculated and the statistical techniques like mean, standard deviation, t-test and ANOVA were used for analyzing and interpreting.

Descriptive analysis for Background information of the selected sample

Differential Analysis

The collected data were consolidated, tabulated and analysed statistically by using the following tests.

1. **Test of Significance ('t' Test and ANOVA)**
2. Mean and Standard Deviation

(1) TEST OF SIGNIFICANCE: 'T' TEST AND ANOVA

't' Test is used to find out the significant level of difference between two groups of population. The values are calculated with the help of the mean scores and standard deviation.

(2) Mean and Standard Deviation

Mean and standard deviation were done using the results of the study to make simple comparisons wherever necessary.

Analysis of 'T' Test Scores of Government Schools Pupil Following the Computer Assisted Instruction

Source	N	Mean	Standard Deviation	t' value'
Pre test Score	50	14.300	3.2467	** 34.799
Post test Score	50	32.22	3.3030	

** Significant at 1% level.

There is no significant difference between the pretest and posttest scores of Government schools pupil following the Computer Assisted Instruction was rejected.

Analysis of 'T' Test Scores of Aided Schools Pupil Following the Computer Assisted Instruction

Source	N	Mean	Standard Deviation	t' value'
Pre test Score	50	15.44	4.6342	** 22.206
Post test Score	50	29.76	4.3451	

** Significant at one percent level.

There is no significant difference between the pretest and posttest scores of Aided Schools Pupil following the Computer Assisted Instruction was rejected.

Analysis of 'T' Test Scores of Unaided Schools Pupil Following the Computer Assisted Instruction

Source	N	Mean	Standard Deviation	t' value'
Pre test Score	50	13.16	3.6048	** 33.969
Post test Score	50	28.98	3.1975	

** Significant at 1% level.

There is no significant difference between the pretest and posttest scores of Unaided Schools Pupil following the Computer Assisted Instruction was rejected.

Significance of Difference between Pre and Post Tests Scores of Computer Assisted Instruction Group

Test	N	Mean	Standard Deviation	t' value'
Pre test	150	14.30	3.9591	** 47.644
Post test	150	30.32	3.8831	

** Significant at 1% level.

There is no significant difference between the pretest and posttest mean scores of the experimental group following CAI was rejected.

Comparison of Posttest Performance of Computer Assisted Instruction Group

Between the Different Type f Schools

Type of the School	N	Mean	Standard Deviation	'F' value
Government School	50	32.22	3.3030	12.824 **
Aided School	50	29.76	4.6451	
Unaided School	50	30.32	3.1975	

** Significant at 1% level.

ANOVA test was applied and the calculated ANOVA value is 12.824, which is found to be significant at 0.01% level. There is no significant difference in posttest performance of Computer Assisted Instruction between the different types of schools pupil was rejected.

Comparison of the Post Test Performance of the Experimental Group Following the CAI with Reference to Locality

Area	N	Mean	Standard Deviation	t' value'
Urban	75	32.00	3.2715	** 5.862
Rural	75	28.64	3.7331	

** Significant at 1% level.

There is no significance difference between posttest performance of Urban and Rural Schools Pupil following the Computer Assisted Instruction was rejected.

Comparison of the Posttest Performance of the Experimental Group following the CAI with Reference to Gender

Gender	N	Mean	Standard Deviation	't' value
Boys	75	29.6567	4.0415	2.084 **
Girls	75	30.9733	3.6279	

** Significant at 5% level.

There is no significance difference between the posttest performance of Boys and Girls following Computer Assisted Instruction was rejected.

SUMMARY OF THE STUDY

The study is an attempt to find out, a comparative study of effectiveness of Computer Assisted Instruction and Handout Instruction on circulatory system for IX standard students.

A sample of 300 pupils studying in IX standard from six different schools in Udumalpet Taluk, Coimbatore District was selected.150 formed of the 300 students experimental group following Computer Assisted Instruction. The experimental method was adopted in the study. Achievement test question paper was employed as a tool, at this time the treatment is administered on a small group of the target population. Pretest and post test are administered prior to starting and after the completion of the treatment respectively. The test scores were taken to assess the effectiveness of self learning through the Computer Assisted Instruction among students.

FINDINGS OF STUDY

The comparison of scores of pretest and post test of Government Schools Pupil following the Computer Assisted Instruction shows significant difference. The mean posttest scores is 32.22 for the Government Schools Pupil which is greater than pretest scores 14.30. This shows the Computer Assisted Instruction significantly influenced learning of pupil.

The mean posttest scores is 29.79 for the Aided Schools Pupil which is greater than pretest scores 15.44. This shows the CAI significantly influenced the learning of Aided Schools Pupil.

The mean posttest scores is 28.98 for unaided schools pupil which is higher than mean pretest scores 13.16. This shows the CAI significantly influenced the learning of unaided schools pupil.

The comparison of the scores of pretest and posttest of overall sample in target group following Computer Assisted instruction shows significant difference. This mean posttest scores is 30.32 for samples which is greater than the mean pretest scores 14.32. This shows CAI significantly influenced learning of all selected samples following CAI.

In this study it was found that same Government Schools has also showing better performance, while they received experimental treatment through CAI when compared to unaided schools and aided schools respectively in post test score.

The comparison of the posttest scores of urban and rural area in the CAI experimental group shows significant difference, the mean value of this CAI experimental group is 32.00 and 28.64 respectively.

Gender wise comparison in the CAI experimental group proved the significant. The calculated 't' value is 2.084. The mean scores of girls are 30.97, which is greater than the mean scores of boys 29.66 in the posttest performances.

RECOMMENDATION

1. Computer assisted instruction should be implemented in more number of the schools.
2. The Government should allot more funds to provide adequate number of computer materials for the schools.
3. It is recommended that Government may give concession for purchase of computer.
4. College students who are studying computer science may be asked to do projects in the development of necessary software for high school syllabus. This can solve the problem of non availability of software.
5. Special training shall be given to the teachers through in-service training

programme to inculcate knowledge about different instructional strategies.

6. Educational institutions should have adequate instructional materials.
7. Training shall be given to the teachers to prepare and handle instrumental materials.
8. Instruction materials of learning provide scope for self instructional activities. Here the role of the teacher is limited and maximum activities are prescribed to the learners.
9. Teacher can improve their competence by attending in service training camps and also by writing research articles in the field of educational technology.
10. The students can learn effectively when they learn on their own. Self learning develops critical thinking in handling of study materials on one's own and enhances communication skills and self reliance.
11. The teachers must motivate the pupils to make more instructional package for self learning.

SUGGESTIONS FOR FURTHER RESEARCH

A Research study would be incomplete if it doesn't provide necessary guidelines as well as potential research topics for further exploration. The following suggestions are made for further research in this area.

1. A similar study can be carried out in different types of school in different parts of Tamil Nadu.
2. In the present study researcher didn't take students from Tamil medium high schools students from such schools can be taken for further study.

CONCLUSION

The density of the country is destined in the classroom. Yes, it is true. The education has a wider meaning now-a-days. The education in the present trend does not mean the mere text book learning. It aims at giving complete life to the pupils. It is more important for the learners to know how to learn rather than what to learn.

From the results of the study, the investigator has ideas of Computer Assisted Instruction provided greater learning opportunities for children both theoretical and practical. Its use in bringing new kinds of experiences for children in school is really interesting and meaningful. The investigator therefore desires that the more number of educational institutions should come forward to make the learning best out of all available instruction materials for learning. So, this amount is just the beginning… not the end.

REFERENCES

1. Aggarwal J.G (1995), Essential of Educational Technology; Teaching Leaning Innovations in Education New Delhi.
2. Bloom, Benjamin S (1956), Taxonomy of Educational Objective Hand books. The cognitive domain. Logmas Publication, New York.
3. Chauhan S.S (1983), Innovations in Teaching Learning Process, New Delhi. Coulson S.E (1962), Programmed Learning and Computer based instruction.
4. David Hawkeridge (1990), New information in Technology and Education, Croomhelm.
5. David Layton (1992), Innovations in Science and Technology Education, Edition III, UNESCO.
6. Ellington, Henry (1985), Producing teaching materials. A Hand book for Teachers and Trainers, London.
7. Forcier (2000) The Computer as a Productivity Tool in Education, Prentice Hall of India.Glass G.V (1970), Statistical method in Education and Psychology, Prentice Hall, Englewood Cliffs.
8. S.P.Gupta (1985), Statistic methods Sultan Chand & Sons Pub. New Delhi. Pp.930.
9. Henry, Ellington, Percival, Fred and Race, Phil (2003), Hand book of Educational Technology, New Delhi. Hemalatha Parasnis, An Orientation to Computer Instruction Experiments in Education. July 1989.
10. John Best. (1963),Research in Education Prentice Hall of India Private Limited, New Delhi.
11. Jaganath Mohanty, Modern Trends in Educational (2003).
12. Kothari C.R (1993), Research Methodology Methods and Techniques.
13. Krishnamoorthy. R (1995) Computer Programming, JJ Publishers, Madurai.
14. Kulkarni (1986), Introduction to Educational Technology, New Delhi. Oxford, IBH Pub.Co.,
15. Mangal S.K (2000), Reversed Edition Foundation of Education Technology.
16. Murthy S.K (1995), Educational Technology Parkash Brothers, Jallandhar.
17. Narayana L.M, A text book of Chordates, Saras Publication, Nagercoil.
18. Palaniappan,V.P.(1990), Effectiveness of Computer Assisted Instruction in Learning Triangles, Media and Technology for Human Resource Development.
19. Pillay, Subramania.G.(1995), Readings in Educational Technology, Nirmal Publication, Madurai.
20. Rajaraman,V.(1985), Fundamentals of Computer, New Delhi, Prentice Hall of India Pvt.Ltd.,
21. Rao B, Anand and Ravishankar. S (1989), Reading in Educational

Technology. Himalaya Publishing House, Bombay.

22. Romesh Verma, Suresh Sharma (1998), Modern Trends in Teaching Technology, Anmol Publications Pvt. Ltd., New Delhi.
23. Sadha and Singh (1982) Methodology of Educational Research, Prentice Hall of India.
24. Sampath and Pannerselvam (1994), Introduction to Educational Technology, Sterling Publishers, New Delhi.
25. Satyanarayana (1985), Research Methodology, Methods and Techniques, Atlantic Pub.
26. Vachan Sing (2005), Practical Approach Educational Technology, Akansha Publishing House, New Delhi.
27. S.Venkataian (2000), Encylopedio of Contemporary Education Series Science Education, Anmol Pub.
28. M.S.Yadav (2000), Modern method of teaching sciences, Anmol Publisher, Delhi.
29. S.M.Zaidi (2004), Modern method of teaching Science, Anmol Publisher, New Delhi.

❐

2.

Competencies - In Using Computers

INTRODUCTION

The information of the twenty first century which has been brought about by advance in the computer technology has created an information society in which majority of labor force are expected to hold and create information related to their jobs. Especially the field of education has been influenced by the increased use of science and technological advancement. This brought changing role of teachers in teacher education too. These facts led the researcher to think and select a problem related to teacher educators' competencies in using computers in their teaching.

RATIONALE

The benefits of technology are general and ICT in particular are beginning to be felt in the development of human resources in administrative and teaching infrastructures. The integration of technology in the classroom is very helpful for students learning (Collins, 1991 and David, 1991) and help learning more interactive (Madian, 1991). Information communications Technologies (ICT) are seen as important tools of advancement in developing countries. As concluded by Duhaney (2000), the introduction and use of ICT changed the traditional classroom activities and changed the way that teachers and students interact with each other. Technologies have proved to have helped enhancing the learning environment and proved enrichment in the learning process (Duhaney, 2000). With the use of technology, the role of the teacher changes such that he/she is no longer the center of the classroom that passes information and knowledge to students.

Students learn through critical thinking, inquiry, and problem solving from information accessed from a variety sources (Houghton, 1997). Many studies have indicated that the reason for the lack of the use of computer technology by teachers is their lack of training (Vagle & College 1995; Yaghi, 1997; Yildirim & Kiraz, 1999). Researchers have shown that teachers are more hesitant and less likely to use computer technology that other people in other professionals (Paprzycki & Vidakovic, 1994). Research into the competency levels of teachers has shown that teacher's beliefs about using technology for teaching are directly related to their practice (Albion, 1999). Research in Scotland indicated that teachers may be aware of their need to gain adequate skills in using ICT but they suffer from lack of time and resources to develop their skills. They depend on other staff to help them through difficulties in using technology (Williams, et al, 1998). On this background researcher developed the following research questions;

RESEARCH QUESTIONS

Specific questions addressed in this study include:

1. To what extent Teacher Educators use Computer applications? If so How frequently do faculty members use computer applications?
2. What are their concerns regarding using technology in teaching?
3. What are faculty members' preferences of technology training methods?

OBJECTIVES

1. To ascertain what extent the Teacher educators have competency in using necessary computer applications and programmes in their teaching.
2. To ascertain the frequency of using computer applications and programmes in their teaching.
3. To ascertain the concerns regarding computer use by teacher educators.
4. To find out the preference mode of training method preferred by them.

TOOLS

1. **Computer competency - survey:** A researcher made survey that consisted of 14 items on a 5 point Likert scale where 1 = Not Competent, and 5 = Highly Competent. These items addressed the use of computer Programs necessary for integrating computer technology in teaching college courses.
2. **Frequency of computer use - survey:** A researcher-made survey that consisted of 14 items for respondent response will be 1= Not at all, and 5 = Always.
3. **Survey on Faculty concern in using computers:** A researcher-made survey that consisted of 11 items that could be of concern to faculty members when using computers.
4. **Survey on the Choice of Computer Training by Faculty Members:** A researcher- made survey that consisted of 4 items that could be of the preferred choice of computer training by faculty members.

PROCEDURE

All those instruments were given to experts for judging their validity. The experts' comments were studied and the instruments were modified accordingly. Therefore the said tools were subjected for its validity through panel judgment. The instruments were distributed among the randomly selected Colleges of Education faculty members' willingness to participate in the research were obtained. About 60 teachers educates were approached randomly and only 50 instruments returned in fully completed form.

Subjects: Table – 1, shows the group (sample) characteristics of the participants taken for this study. The participants for this study were 50 faculty members working in the various colleges of Education in Puducherry region (randomly) during the academic year 2011-2012.

Table - 1

Characteristics		**Number**	**%**
Sex	Male	28	56
	Female	22	44
Age	21-30yrs	18	36
	31-40yrs	20	40
	41-50yrs	07	14
	51-60yrs	05	10
Faculty	B.Ed. Level	35	70
	M.Ed. Level	15	30
Computer access	At home	32	64
	At College Library	18	36
Internet access	At home	15	30
	At College Library	18	36
	Not using	17	34

DATA ANALYSIS

The data collected from the 50 participants were subjected to descriptive statistics of mean and standard deviation for the instruments 1 and 2 and total scores in percentage were calculated for the instruments 3 and 4.

RESULTS AND DISCUSSION

Table 2. Computer Competency: Descriptive Statistics

S.No	ITEM	1.COMPUTER COMPETENCY		2.FREQUENCY OF USE	
		Mean (Max=5)	Std. Deviation	Mean (Max=5)	Std. Deviation
1	Internet and WWW	2.68	1.15	2.88	1.19
2	Electronic Mail	3.4	1.09	2.86	1.02
3	Presentation Software (eg. Power Point, Adobe Captivate, Adobe Presenter, author STREAM, e-learning suite)	3.18	1.04	1.3	0.65
4	Word Processing (Eg. Word 2003,2007,2010)	3.66	1.06	1.2	0.44
5	Slide Projection (using LCD, Slide projector)	3.02	0.98	1.98	0.59
6	Transparencies (with OHP)	3.7	0.88	3.86	0.71
7	Spread Sheets (eg. Excel)	3.34	1.31	1.9	0.70
8	Statistical Analysis (eg. Spss, other free, online statistical softwares)	1.7	1.06	1.12	0.30
9	Data base software (eg. Student data base access, other data bases)	2.4	0.91	1.14	0.33
10	Audio Editing Programs (eg. Audacity)	1.06	0.30	1.06	.24
11	Video Editing Programs (Video Editing softwares & utilities)	1.1	0.25	1.1	.34
12	Digital Drawing Programs (eg. Photoshop)	1	0	1	0
13	Animation software programms (eg.Flash)	1	0	1	0
14	Web design programs (creating and maintaining)	1	0	1	0

The result on the computer competency survey are shown table 2 - a. Computer competency. The means on the 14 items ranged from 1 (Web design programs) to 3.66 (Word Processing). The result shows that 3.66 for Word Processing skill and 3.34 for Spread Sheet skill used much than any other area of computer competency.

Whereas the item no 8 to 14 are not used considerably and regularly. The reason must be due to lack of knowledge, access or other reasons involved. The Items 1 & 9 indicating an intermediate level of competency. These results suggest that faculty members need training on tools other than these tools to raise their level of competency. On the rest of items, however, the means are less than 1, which means that faculty members are at low level of competency on these tools. Therefore, a large dose of training is required on the use of these tools usage.

The result on the Computer frequency of uses such technology by the faculty members shown as in table 2. The means on the 14 items ranged from 1 (Web design programs, Animation software programs, Digital Drawing Programs, Video Editing Programs, Audio Editing Programs, Data base, Statistical Analysis software and Word Processing) to 3.8 (Transparencies) (Internet and WWW, Electronic Mail) . The bottom 8 items (see table-2) where not used by faculty members, because of lack of knowledge, due to lack of facilities to make use of it. On the other hand, it is reasonable to assume that one would use programs that he/ she is good at using it. The means of the item 1,2 &6 were less than 2. This means that many important computer applications are not utilized for educational use or for personal use.

Table-4. Main concerns of Faculty Members in Using Technology

S.No.	Common Concerns	Yes%	No%
1	No technical support	85	15
2	No time	55.5	44.5
3	Need new computer	75.5	24.5
4	No infrastructure (Equipment and Software)	90	10
5	Difficulties in using technology	67	33
6	No incentives	48	52
7	The cost of using technology	84	16
8	Student might be better than me	43	57
9	Not enough ability	40	60
10	Does not know how to use Internet	58.1	41.9
11	Don't think student will learn this way	19.1	80.9

Table-4 shows faculty members answers to the items representing their concern regarding computer use. It can be concluded from the table 3 that the common problems that faculty members reported are no Technical support, not having enough time, need new computer, no proper equipment and software and difficulties in using technology. 19.1% of faculty members are of the opinion that they don't think students will learn through computers. This may be negative attitude towards computers or due to lack of exposure to computer applications in education.

Table-5. Analyis of the choice of training by faculty members

S.No.	Traning Type	First in %	Second in %	Third in %
1	Workshop	58.5	20.6	11.4
2	Peer	12.7	22.6	35.9
3	One to One	14.9	22.7	20.9
4	Manual	13.9	34.1	31.8
	Total	100	100	100

Table–5, shows the faculty members' preferences of computer training methods. It can be noticed that most of the faculty members' first choice was workshops, second choice was the one to one training strategy and the third choice was to provide them a manual that would be taught.

RECOMMENDATIONS FOR POLICY MAKING

1. Technologies in general and ICT in particular offer vast opportunities for the development of contacts and exchange of information and knowledge with the rest of the world. Incorporating the technologies successfully in educational institutions requires careful advanced planning and preparation. Significant finance and human resources are required, with training as an essential to be prepared to confront bureaucracy and conservative attitudes, including resistance by teachers and other educational staff. The following recommendations may help educational policy makers to incorporate and utilize ICT for education and training in a productive manner:
2. Training and orientation of teachers, administrators and students to the new learning technologies is an immediate requirement.
3. Teachers should have adequate time to plan the introduction of ICT into their pedagogical practices to ensure high quality and appropriate learning.
4. Broadening awareness of a wide range of ICT resources, with equal emphasis on word processing, presentation software like power point, spreadsheets like excel and on resources which are currently underused, such as the internet and WWW, e-mail, and video conferencing, e-teaching, e-learning, blogging etc.,

5. Training must be focused on the development of "ICT competencies on teacher educators"
6. Providing opportunities for continuing professional development in ICT

TEACHER EDUCATOR' INITIATIVES FOR ICT INTEGRATION

Whatever may be the inputs in the training and however well designed it is, the transformation can't be achieved without the leadership, commitment and initiatives of the teachers and teacher educators, both could take up initiatives like:

1. Self-learning using the tutorials available on the net, or print medium.
2. Hiring an ICT expert by a group of teacher/teacher educators to teach them.
3. Enrolling for online professionally development courses. There are many websites offering free training modules.
4. Enrolling for the best commercially available ICT training programs.
5. Coaching by a colleague-Mentoring.
6. Attending ICT training courses, seminars, conferences and workshops.
7. Communities of teachers' collaborative groups to integrate ICT into their curriculum (same projects, different subjects, same school/college, different school/college)
8. Online learning by means of videoconferencing, discussion forum, chat, blogging etc.,
9. Visiting institutions where the ICT IS ALREADY BEING INTEGRATED
10. ACTION RESEARCH trying out various models of technology integration and publishing the result of the same.
11. Membership and active participation in national and international associations, whose primary concern is technology.
12. Take up diploma or certificate courses on ICT offered through distance mode by national or international universities and organizations. The University of HULL currently offers a course M.Ed., in E-learning through online mode. (http:/ces.hull.ac.uk/courses/MedineLearning.html)
13. Keeping up to date with the latest developments in ICT through journals, magazines, newspapers and the internet.
14. Teacher educators who modeling the ICT integration in their academic work.
15. Planning and implementing ICT in-service training programs for school teachers the best way to learn is to teach.
16. Creating a pool of ICT competent past teacher trainees and involving them in the training programs.
17. Designing and implementing self financing certificate course in ICT for in-service teachers.
18. ICT should not be restricted to a single course but needs to permeate in all courses in the programmes.(UNESCO)

CONCLUSION

Educational technology is not, and never will be, transformational on its own. Technology can play a critical role in creating new circumstances and opportunities for learning that can be rich and exciting. Technology can facilitate deep exploration and integration of information, high-level thinking and profound engagement by allowing students to design, explore, experiment, access information, and model complex phenomena. Particularly in Teacher training the Trainee Students should experience innovative technology supported learning environment in Teacher-Education programmes. Otherwise they cannot have opportunities to equip them to make use of the same while they go into the regular stream as a teacher.

REFERENCES

1. Albion, P. (1999). Self-efficacy Beliefs as an Indicator of Teachers' Preparedness for Teaching with Technology, Association for the Advancement of Computing in Education,
2. Collins, A. (1991). The role of computer technology in restructuring schools. Phi Delta Kappan, 73(1), 28-36).
3. David, J.(1991) Restructuring and technology: Partners in change. Phi Delta Kappan,73(1),37-40).
4. Duhaney, D. C (2000). Technology and the Educational Process: transforming classroom activities, International Jouranl of Insttructional Media, 27(1), 67-72.
5. Houghton, M. (1997). Sate strategies for incorporating technology into education. Washington, DC: National Governers' Association. (ERIC No. ED 412 930).
6. Madian, j. (1991). Technology's place in curriculum reform. ISTE update, 3(7), 1-2.
7. Paprzycki, M & Vidakovic, D. (2994). Prospective teacher's attitude towards computers, In D.Willis,B.Rovin,&J.Willis (Eds.)Technology and Teacher Traning Annual.1994 (pp.74-76).
8. Vagle, R, & College, D (1995). Technology instruction for preservice teachers: An examination of excemplary programs, In D. Wilis, B, Robin, & J. Willis (Eds.,) Technology and teacher education annual-1995 (pp-230-237).
9. Williams, D., Wilson, K, Richardson, A., Tuson, J and Coles, L (1998) Teachers' ICT skills and knowlede Needs; final reprot to SOEID, School of Information and Media Faculty of Management, the Robert Gordon Univerisity, Scotland, Http://WWW.scotland. Gov.uk./library/ict/append-section5.htm
10. Anjali Khirwadhat, R.L.Madhv, (2006) 'ICT in education, An integrated approach" Edutracks, pg.14-17 July, 2006.

11. Sharad Sinha (2006) 'Technology Integration –Issues and Challenges" Journal of all India Association for Educational Research, vol 18, nos3 &4, Sep.&Dec.2006.
12. M.U.Paily, (2006) 'Integration of ICT in Teacher Education" Edutracks, Vol5 no.6 pg.5-11, Feb., 2006.Steketee Carole, "Integrating ICT as an integral teaching and learning tool into preservice teacher training courses."

❐

3.

Cloud Computing and Access to Public Services among the Teacher Trainees of Special Education Programme

INTRODUCTION

Network-based services, which appear to be provided by real server hardware and are in fact served up by virtual hardware simulated by software running on one or more real machines, is often called cloud computing.

Student often search the materials through internet to update their knowledge. People stated doing their business by sitting at their hose. We make all our planning with the help of computer, laptop or mobiles connected to internet. Any kind of services are available at door step by clicking a mouse.

An attempt is made to study the accessibility of public services among the teacher trainees of Special Education College through cloud computing in their academic and day to day life.

Network-based services, which appear to be provided by real server hardware and are in fact served up by virtual hardware simulated by software running on one or more real machines, is often called cloud computing.

Cloud computing is computing that involves a large number of computers connected through a communication net work such as the internet, similar to utility computing. In science cloud computing is a synonym for distributed computing over a net work, and means the ability to run a programme or application on many connected computers at a same time.

The cloud computing was available via thin clients /terminal computers known as static terminals in the beginning. Later it becomes time sharing in the industry and in 70's it become Remote job Entry process associated with IBM and Others.

The term cloud computing is mostly used to sell hosted services in the sense of application service provisioning that run client server software at a remote location. Such services are given with the acronyms of 'SaaS' (Software as a Service) 'PaaS' (Platform as a Service), 'IaaS' (Infrastructure as a Service), HaaS (Hardware as a Service), and finally, EaaS' (Everything as a Service)

End users access cloud based applications through a web browser, thin client or mobile applications, while the business software and users data are stored on servers at a remote location.

This cloud services may be offered in a public private or hybrid net work Amazon Web services, Google apple engine, Oracle Zoho and Azure are some of the venders. This allocate space for a user to deploy and manage software "in the cloud" The client devices of cloud computing are desk top computers, laptops, tablets and smart phones.

With the help of cloud computing Searching study materials, Results, E-banking, E-ticketing, E-Payment are common now and that becomes part of our life.

This study will focus on the accessibility of cloud computing for availing the public services by the student trainees undergoing teacher training programme in a special education college for their academic and other personnel use.

REVIEW OF LITERATURE

Jake Gardner explains that while unregulated usage is beneficial for IT and tech moguls like Amazon, the anonymous nature of the cost of consumption of cloud usage make it difficult for business to evaluate and incorporate it in to their business plan.

1. Slovoj Zizek points out that although cloud computing enhances content accessibility this access is increasingly grounded in the virtually monopolistic privatization of the cloud which provide this access.
2. Zizek criticizes the argument purported by the supporters of cloud computing that this phenomenon is part of the natural evaluation of the internet sustaining that the quasi monopolies yet prices at will but also filter the software they provide to give its universality a particular twist depending on commercial and ideological interests.
3. European commission (2012) has issued an analysis of the relevance of the open research issues for commercial stabilization in which various experts from industry and academia identify in particular following major concerns 1.Open interoperation across (proprietary) cloud solutions at IaaS, PaaS and SaaS levels 2. Managing multi tenancy at large scale and

in heterogeneous environments 3.Dynamic and seamless elasticity from in house clouds to public clouds for unusual (scale, complexity) and/or infrequent requirements 4.Data management in a cloud environment, taking the technical and legal constraints into consideration.

4. Johnson (2013) reported that Virtualization and cloud orchestrian turned a corner here to take virtualization to its logical conclusion of allowing business users to access their desktops from any laptop, tablet or smartphone.
5. Newman (2013). Reported that the new programming of elastic computer cloud may change the carbon and electricity cost of developing cloud computing and minimize the wastages.
6. Rozenfeld.M.(2013) Stated that as we become more reliant on mobile phones and tablets, central storage of data and fast access to systems in the cloud become essential to enable ubiquitous and anytime access. To these ends, the technologies that support the cloud must become faster, more cost-effective, and more secure.
7. Xu.J.S.etall (2013) developed a model to service document mechanism which will protect the security of the programme in the cloud computing.

Aim

This study will aim to understand the use of cloud computing with the teacher trainees in their academic and their personal works.

Objective

To find out the application of cloud computing as a supportive programme for academic works of the student trainees.

1. To find out the use of cloud computing in their day to day life.

Method

Survey method.

Sampling

Purposive sampling, 71 student trainees from a teacher training college offering special education programme is selected for this study.

Tool

A questionnaire consisting of 20 items comprising of the use of personal computer, laptop and mobile which is connected to internet for searching the educational materials, booking tickets, and availing other services at college, home and other places were developed for administering on the individuals.

Procedure

The tool is given to individuals and requested to give their response on each item by scoring (2) for frequently used (1) for occasionally used (0) for never used against to the question.

Result and Discussion

After obtaining the response from the student trainees the scores were tabulated and reported

From the table it is revealing that access to study materials using computes at college is more than that of at any other places. Accessing the study materials using laptop seems to be more at home that that of at any other places. Accessing the study material using cell phones is very minimal.

Accessing the exam result through internet is more common with the students. Ticket booking for their travel also fairly observes with the students.

Very few students are accessing internet for other purposes like banking, shopping submission of online applications and chatting with others.

Table I: Cloud computing and access to public services among the teacher trainees of a special education college.

Sl.No.		Diploma			Degree			PG			Total
		Not Used	Rare	Frequent	Not Used	Rare	Frequent	Not Used	Rare	Frequent	
1	computer at college	22	22	02	09	11	00	03	00	02	71
2	computer at home	40	04	02	16	03	01	02	00	03	71
3	computer outside	36	09	01	12	04	04	04	01	00	71
4	laptop at college	44	02	00	18	01	01	05	00	00	71
5	laptop at home	41	04	01	16	03	01	03	00	02	71
6	laptop outside	40	04	02	11	09	00	04	01	00	71
7	cellphone at college	37	07	02	17	00	03	03	01	01	71
8	cellphone at home	36	05	05	12	04	04	04	01	00	71
9	cellphone outside	40	05	01	14	06	00	04	01	00	71
10	online shopping	46	00	00	16	04	00	04	00	01	71
11	online banking	46	00	00	16	03	01	03	01	01	71
12	online payment	45	01	00	18	02	00	03	01	01	71
13	e-money order	46	00	00	19	01	00	05	00	00	71
14	online business	45	01	00	19	01	00	04	00	01	71
15	online movie reservation	42	03	01	15	05	00	04	00	01	71

16	online journey reservation	44	02	00	12	08	00	01	02	02	71
17	online doctor appointment	46	00	00	16	04	00	05	00	00	71
18	online application submission	40	06	00	13	04	03	03	00	02	71
19	online exam	42	04	00	13	05	02	04	00	01	71
20	online result	33	12	01	01	14	05	02	01	02	71
21	online game	43	03	00	08	10	02	05	00	00	71
22	online communication	37	09	00	08	09	03	01	02	02	71

Postgraduate students are accessing more public services through cloud computing followed by the degree and diploma students. Statistically there is no significant difference observed in this study

Conclusion

The personal computer is very supportive for student trainees to collect the study materials in the college. The laptop is useful for the trainees tot store and does the review at home. The mobile phone is used for commercial business. The government is providing laptop to the student further it needs to be connected with clouding system so that the public service will be accessed easily.

This study is limited and there is a need of conducting more study on identifying the needs of student to access the public services.

Recommendations

Every college needs to provide the wi-fi facilities to access the public services to the students

Government can bring out a scheme of access to internet facilities to laptop issued at school so that the public services can be availed at any movement.

Reference

1. "The NIST Definition of Cloud Computing "(2011) National Institute of Standards and Technology Retrieved 24 July 2011.
2. What is cloud computing Amazon Web Services 2013-03-19 Retrieved 2013-03-20.
3. Baburajan, Rajani (2011). The raising cloud storage market opportunity strengthens Vendors info tech it.tmc.net.com 2011 -07-24 retrieved 2011 -12-02
4. Dan Sullivan (2014) Cost of the cloud a developers guide to reducing your Bill Retrieved 2014 -11-27
5. Sinmon Garfrinkel 2011) The cloud imperative technology review (MIT)

Retrieved 31 May 2013.

6. Danielson, Krissi (2008-03-26). "Distinguishing Cloud Computing from Utility Computing". Ebizq.net. Retrieved 2010-08-22
7. Rozenfeld .M.(2013) Bridging the gap in the cloud paper presented in the conference on how silicon system can lead to a more mobile and connected world. In San Francisco
8. Xu.J.S.etall (2013) Secure document service for cloud computing University of Post and Telecommunication China.

❐

4.

Effectiveness of E-Content in Teaching

INTRODUCTION

The development of Science and Technology, especially the application of information and communication technology (ICT) in the new era has greatly influenced teaching and learning in education. In the present era of knowledge explosion, adopting modern tools for teaching is one of the predominant needs of the hour. Instructional technology in the third world is changing rapidly. Knowledge packaging in electronic form or e-content is a powerful technique for teaching all subjects. ICT have become handy in class room teaching which has the potential to engage the students throughout the period and make learning easy and effective through, visual aids, animations and simulations.

NEED FOR THE STUDY

New innovations are coming to the fields of education in terms of technology which promises to change the process of teaching and learning. Training of competent teachers is very important because they directly or indirectly influence the quality and the quantity of educational services. Without adequately trained teacher cadre the institution cannot aim to expand the educational facilities.

E-CONTENT

The term 'e-content' refers to that form of knowledge or content which is packed in an electronic form. It includes text, audio, video, animations, images etc. An innovative application of computer in the teaching and learning process is e-content. E-content is the advancement of technology to design, deliver, select, administer and extend learning.

OBJECTIVES OF THE STUDY

1. To prepare e-content for particular topic in Teaching of Biological Science Education at B.Ed., level.
2. To find out whether there is any significant difference in achievement means score between control group and experimental group in learning Teaching of Biological Science Education by the B.Ed., student teachers.

METHODOLOGY

The investigator followed the experimental method for the present study. The data thus collected were put into appropriate statistical analysis: Mean, t-test, standard deviation.

SAMPLING PROCEDURE

The present study is concerned only with B.Ed student teachers in J.J. College of Education and Oxford College of Education, Trichy. Hence the college selected could be considered as a representative college. Eighteen students have been selected for experimental group and another eighteen students for control group by using purposive sampling method.

HYPOTHESES OF THE STUDY

The following hypotheses were formulated based on the objectives of the study

1. There is no significant difference in the Posttest achievement mean scores between control group and experimental group.
2. There is significant difference in the achievement mean scores between the Pre and Post test of experimental groups who learnt through e-content.

Table 1: The table shows the comparison of Post-test achievement mean scores of Experimental group and control group.

Group Compared	N	M	SD	't' value	df	Level of significance
Control Group	18	8.72	1.127	9.22	34	**Significant**
Experimental Group	18	13.33	1.910			

The calculated t-value 9.22 is greater than the critical value 2.704 corresponding to the 0.01 level of significance. This implies that the control group and experimental group differ significantly in their achievement in the post-test. Hence the null hypothesis is not accepted.

Table 2: The table shows the difference between the Pre-test and Post-test achievement mean scores due to treatment for the experimental group.

Experimental Group	No of students	Mean	SD	't' value	df	Level of significance
Pre – test	18	10.72	1.364	8.040	34	**Significant**
Post - test	18	13.33	1.910			

The calculated t-value 8.040 is greater than the critical value 2.704 corresponding to the 0.01 level of significance. This shows that experimental group is highly significant in their achievement in post-test. Hence the null hypothesis is accepted.

MAJOR FINDINGS OF THE STUDY

The major findings which have emerged from the study are as follows:

1. An Achievement test was conducted to access the effectiveness of the e-content. While analyzing the result, i.e., the performance of the students in the achievement test is better and it became clear that the e-content is effective.
2. The student teachers of experimental group who were taught through e-content achieved more in subject units than the control group student teachers.
3. It was found .that learning through e-content and learning through traditional lecture method are not similar and they differ significantly.

EDUCATIONAL IMPLICATIONS OF THE STUDY

1. New instructional techniques of assisting student through computer are to be explored by the teachers and researchers continuously.
2. Teachers of higher secondary schools can be given orientation as how to develop e-content.
3. The use of e-content is found to be valid in enhancing the achievement; it will diminish wastage and stagnation in school.

CONCLUSION

Based on the proceeding findings of the study, the following conclusions are arrived. The levels of performance of teacher trainees who learnt through e-content were greater the other part and hence it was evident that e-content is also an effective approach to teach Biological Science Education. The rise of e-learning and an electronic content (e-content) is a new paradigm for education and training in the knowledge society, empowered by technological advancements which give the modern instructional technology. The development of educational content in time with the changing times has become a major responsibility of the modern teacher who has to face a new learner in a new environment. More over the level of motivation, learning style and anxiety towards computer improves the efficiency of the student teachers and hence the e-content approach is having great scope in the instructional design of the student teachers.

REFERENCES

1. Jeya Shanmuga Raja. J, E-Content Development on Teaching method of Zoology at B.Ed Level., Paper presented at the International conference on Quality Enhancement in Distance Education for LifeLong Learning 26-27 March 2011,
2. Suma.S.(2007). Development and Validation of e-content on the uses of the simple present tense in English at higher secondary level. M.Phil Thesis submitted to Bharathidasan University.
3. Udayakumar.P, Impact of Multimedia Technology in Learning Biological Science on B.Ed. Trainees, http://www.languageinindia.com/feb2013/udayakumarfinal.pdf saved on 14.5.13

❐

5.

Awareness of Computer Utilization among the Prospective Teachers

INTRODUCTION

The present century is rightly called the technological century. The development in various aspects of computer technology has reached beyond our imagination and expectations. Science and technology play a significant role in the formation of modern civilization in any society. The increasing scientific and technological impact upon human life activities is developing the scientific attitude of people.

NEED FOR THE STUDY

The awareness of computer helps the teacher to appreciate and adopt emerging communication technology and innovative practices. It provides guidance for the development of a high quality strategies technology plan. It enables the teacher to update the new knowledge and skill to use the new digital tools and resources. Improving the quality of education through diversification of contents and methods and promoting experimentation, innovation and sharing of information are UNESCO's strategic objectives in education. So the teachers must have the skill of using computer further, the students of bachelor of education can acquire the knowledge of computer, so that they can become effective teachers. Hence, investigator has taken the following topic for his investigation.

STATEMENT OF THE PROBLEM

"Awareness of Computer Utilization among the Prospective Teachers in Tirunelveli District"

OPERATIONAL DEFINITIONS

Awareness

It is a process of acquiring knowledge about computer.

Computer

It is the scientific and technological discipline which deals with collection, Strong and dissemination of information to the individuals.

Awareness of Computer

It is the process of knowing the function of computer, operations of computer, Utilization of computer and uses of computer-how they work, how they help to solve the Problem of today's world.

Utilization

Utilization means the act of using. Prefers hear using the computer,internet,website and e-mail etc.

Prtospective Teachers

Students those who are studying Bachelor of education, after finishing their Graduation.

GENERAL OBJECTIVES OF THE STUDY

Following are the objectives of the present study.

1. To find out the level of the awareness of computer utilization among the prospective teachers with respect to background variables
2. To find out whether there is any significant different awareness of computer utilization among the prospective teachers with respect to background variables

REVIEW OF RELATED LITERATURE

Galanouli and McNair (2001), conducted a study on "students' perceptions of ICT-related pedagogic support in teaching placements".

Recent research has shown that students' use of information and communications technology (ICT) on teaching practice is necessary for effective future use of ICT in the classroom. All 110 students-teachers attending one university's eight postgraduate certificates in education (PGCE) courses completed a questionnaire on their attitudes to ICT in learning and teaching and their initial experiences of the application of ICT in schools. In-depth interviews with the students-teachers, as well as university tutors and teachers, revealed a range of issues that reflected how students-teachers perceive their school-based ICT training and what they think could improve their experiences. Recommendations are offered for the improvement of the ICT school experiences for students-teachers until teacher training is completed and improved ICT infrastructure is in place in schools. The overriding conclusion is that schools must be supported and resourced properly, and teachers must have effective ICT training, before improvements in school-based ICT development for student-teachers can be achieved.

METHOD USED IN THE STUDY

The investigator used a survey method for the study.

POPULATION FOR THE STUDY

The population of the study includes the students of B.Ed. course in Tirunelveli District.

SAMPLE FOR THE STUDY

The investigator has used simple random sampling technique for selecting the colleges under Tamil Nadu Teacher's Education University, Chennai. The investigator selected the B.Ed., Colleges in Tirunelveli District. Investigator selected 300 B.Ed. students from 6 colleges in this district, giving importance to gender and location of colleges.

TOOLS USED IN THE PRESENT STUDY

Awareness of computer utilization among the prospective teachers scale developed by the investigator with the help of a guide

STATISTICAL TECHNIQUES USED IN THE PRESENT STUDY

The investigators have used the following statistical techniques

1. Percentage Analysis
2. Arithmetic Mean
3. Standard Deviation
4. 't' test
5. 'F' test

Null hypothesis 1

There is no significant difference between rural and urban prospective teachers in their awareness of computer utilization and its dimensions.

Significant Difference between Rural and Urban Prospective Teachers in Their Awareness of Computer Utilization and Its Dimensions

Dimension	Variation	Mean	S.D	't' value	Remarks
Computer awareness	Rural	48.44	6.038	0.14	NS
	Urban	48.30	6.947		
Internet awareness	Rural	49.48	6.735	0.34	NS
	Urban	49.84	6.708		
E-mail awareness	Rural	51.99	7.688	0.50	NS
	Urban	52.58	6.825		

Website awareness	Rural	53.50	7.263	1.97	S
	Urban	55.18	5.082		
Awareness of computer	Rural	203.41	23.608	0.68	NS
	Urban	205.90	22.568		

(At 5% level of significance, the table value of 't' is 1.96)

Null hypothesis 2

There is no significant association between father's education and their awareness of computer utilization among the prospective teachers.

The 'χ^2' Value between Father's Education and their Awareness of Computer Utilization among the Prospective Teachers

Dimension	Father's Education	Low	Moderate	High	Calculated 'χ^2' values	Remarks
Computer awareness	Illiterate	17	43	11	2.53	NS
	School	44	102	46		
	Degree	8	22	7		
Internet awareness	Illiterate	17	47	7	9.76	S
	School	47	104	41		
	Degree	9	17	11		
E-mail awareness	Illiterate	15	42	14	1.84	NS
	School	44	100	48		
	Degree	8	18	11		
Website awareness	Illiterate	16	42	13	2.59	NS
	School	47	106	39		
	Degree	12	16	9		
Awareness of computer	Illiterate	17	36	18	0.39	NS
	School	48	98	46		
	Degree	10	17	10		

(At 5% level of significance, the table value of 'χ^2' at 4 df is 9.488)

FINDINGS

1. There is no significant difference between rural and urban prospective teachers in their computer awareness, internet awareness, e-mail awareness, website awareness and the awareness of computer utilization among the prospective teachers in total.

2. There is no significant association between father education of prospective teachers of in their computer awareness, e-mail awareness, website awareness and the awareness of computer utilization among the prospective teachers in total. But there is a significant difference in their internet awareness.

INTERPRETATIONS

The 't' test result reveals that the urban students are better than rural students in their website awareness. This may be due to the fact that the urban prospective teachers have more facilities for study than the rural prospective teachers. So the website awareness is higher than the prospective teachers are urban students.

The 'χ^2' result reveals that there is significant association between father's education of B.Ed. students and their internet awareness. This may be due to the fact that father's with more educational knowledge are able to use the internet awareness in a better way. They schedule the work and delegate people according to the nature of work. Their education helps them to uses people according to their requires needs.

RECOMMENDATIONS

1. In B.Ed. Course along with regular programs, seminars, workshops and symposium on awareness of computer can be conducted.
2. B.Ed. trainees can be trained to teach their lessons using power point presentations.
3. Teacher education training should familiarize the future teachers with various innovative methods and strategies to teach effectively.
4. Internet based teaching can be followed in B.Ed. colleges.

SUGGESTIONS

1. The similar type of studies can be extended to other schools, colleges and universities exploring the same field of investigation.
2. Relationship between awareness of computer and academic achievement of the college students may be conducted.
3. A study of relationship between awareness of computer and teaching effectiveness of college professors may be conducted.
4. A study of relationship between awareness of computer and teaching effectiveness of secondary teacher education may be conducted.

CONCLUSION

From the above study, we conclude that awareness of computer utilization among the prospective teachers is moderate. By giving computer related seminars, symposium, and workshop to student teacher. We can improve their efficiency in teaching, so this is the right time to study about this topic to give excellence among the B.Ed. college students.

REFERENCES

1. Aggarwal J.C (1986) 'Education Research', Arya Book Depot, New Delhi.
2. Aggarwal Y.P (2002) 'Statistical Methods, Concepts, ApplicationAnd Computation', Arya Book Depot, New Delhi.
3. Lalini Varanasi, Sudhakar.V, And Murunalini (2005) 'Computer Education',Neelkamal Publications Pvt.Ltd,Newdelhi.

❐

6.

Effectiveness of Educational Software on Achievement in Chemistry among Students of Standard XI

INTRODUCTION

The instruction through Educational Software has been making wonders in the class room activities. 'Eureka Educational Software' has developed Educational Software in the name of "Designmate" for different subjects such as Mathematics, Physics, Chemistry and Biology for the Standards from VI to XII. More animations and interactions are incorporated in this Software. The Investigator wanted to know, the effectiveness of the Eureka Educational Software on the Achievement in Chemistry. Hence the Investigators were aimed to study the Effectiveness of Educational Software on Achievement in Chemistry among the Students of Standard XI. The study belongs to an Experimental Research. The sample of the study based on the half – yearly performance of the students, they are divided into two groups. The total number of students 79, of which 37 belonged to Control Group and 42 belonged to Experimental Group. The Eureka Educational Software "Designmate" was the Dependent Variable and the Achievement in Chemistry was the Independent Variable. The developed Achievement Test in Chemistry by the Investigator was conducted before and after the treatment for both Control and Experiment Groups. Then the Investigator taught Chemistry through Educational Software to the Experimental Group. Similar topics in Chemistry were taught through Lecture Method to the Control Group. The collected data was analysed by using different statistical techniques such as Mean, Standard Deviation and 't' test. The study found that the Achievement made through Educational Software by Experimental Group was significantly higher than the Control Group.

Computer Assisted Instruction (CAI) has emerged as an effective and efficient media of instruction in the advanced countries of the world. CAI is being used in the formal and non-formal educations at all levels. In India too computer has been introduced in most of the areas such as data processing, decision making, etc., it has impact on the working methods of research and development in the field of Science and Technology. First CAI attempt was made around 1961 when University of Illinois produced Programmed Logic for Automatic Teaching Operation (PLATO). Hence, the use of computer in general education started from early sixties. The Computer Assisted or Aided Instruction may be defined as the use of computer as an integral part of an instructional system, the learner generally engaging in two – way interaction with the computer via terminal.

"Designmate', is a Educational Software developed by Eureka Educational Software which is a 17 years old Multimedia Production House, involved into various activities like making of interactive presentation, animated films, music videos, special effects. They are the first people in India to do a full four minute animated music video where a live character interacts and dance with a computer generated character Anaida's " Hoo Halla Hoo". They received an award for Best Animation from Autodesk. Eureka Educational Software developed 'Designmate', which were converting the entire textbooks into colourful 3D animated movies with interactive games and puzzles. Bringing a visually beautiful and interesting learning experience, enhancing the student's learning and retention capabilities. This Education Software was distributed to Schools via Server and LAN. This Education Software covers Science and Mathematics subjects from class VI to XII.

OBJECTIVES OF THE STUDY

The objectives of the study are:

1. To find out the significant difference between the Pre – Test Scores of the Control and Experimental group.
2. To find out the significant difference between the Post – Test Scores of the Control and Experimental group.
3. To find out the significant difference between Control and Experimental group at the Pre – Test and Post – Test Scores.
4. To find out the effect of Educational Software on Achievement in Chemistry with respect to different variables such as of Gender, Caste and Science Marks secured in Standard X.

HYPOTHESES

The following hypotheses were formulated to realize the above objectives.

1. There is no significant difference between the Pre- Test and Post-Test Scores of the Control group and Experimental group.
2. There is no significant difference between the Control group and Experimental group at the Pre – Test and Post – Test Scores.
3. There is no influence of Gender, Caste and Science Marks secured in Standard X (SMSX) over the effect of Educational Software on Achievement in Chemistry.

NATURE OF THE RESEARCH

The present investigation is Experimental in nature, because the investigators aimed to compare the Effectiveness of Teaching Chemistry to the XI Standard Students through Teaching and through Eureka Educational Software.

SAMPLE SELECTION

The investigators selected XI Standard Students of Periyar Centenary Memorial Matriculation Higher Secondary School, K.K.Nagar Trichy to carry out the Experiment because the School has been posed with well equipped computer facilities. Based on the half-yearly performance of the Students, they are divided into two groups. The total number of students 79, of which 37 belonged to Control Group and 42 belonged to Experimental Group.

DEVELOPMENT OF TOOL

The Eureka Educational Software, 'Designmate' was the Dependent Variable and the Achievement in Chemistry was the Independent Variable. The Eureka Educational Software was given to the Post Graduate Teachers who are handling Chemistry in the nearby schools for content validity. The opinion of them was highly satisfactory.

The developed Achievement test questionnaires were framed by the investigators with the guidance of the subject experts covering the following items such as Knowledge, Understanding, Application and Skill. These questionnaires were validated by Test – Retest method among the Student of XI Standard. The developed Achievement Test in Chemistry was conducted before and after the treatment for both Control and Experiment Groups. Then the Investigators taught Chemistry through Educational Software to the Experimental Group. Similar topics in Chemistry were taught through Lecture Method to the Control Group.

After the finalization of the tool, the investigators had given 40 items to the Students. Each item was in the form of multiple choices with an incomplete statement. For each item four alternative answers were given. Only one was the correct answer. The Students were requested to write the response in the form of correct alpha bate a, b, c and d. Each × responses carry 1 mark.

DATA ANALYSIS

Thus the data collected in this manner undertake analysis by using different statistical technique. Mean and SD were calculated for each Variables to calculate 't' values which is the test of significance of the difference between two means. The following tables contained the data regarding the Control group and Experimental group with the following variables such as Gender, Caste and SMSX.

Table 1: Mean and SD of the Student towards Achievement Score for different Category of Control Group

Sl.No	Variable	Category	Sample Size	Mean		SD	
				Pre-Test	Post-Test	Pre-Test	Post-Test
01.	Gender	Boys	18	20.83	65.97	9.09	13.31
		Girls	19	15.53	62.5	12.05	17.37
02.	Caste	OC/BC	23	22.07	65.43	11.48	16.57
		MBC/SC/ST	14	11.61	62.14	6.09	13.69
03.	SMSX	Above 70%	21	21.55	68.21	10.73	11.34
		Below 70%	16	13.59	62.66	9.72	16.31
04.	Total		37	18.11	64.19	11.03	15.63

From the above table 1 it is revealed that the average Mean Score of the Student towards Achievement Score for different category is 18.11 at Pre – Test level and 64.19 at Post – Test level which show the effectiveness of Lecture Method. Moreover at the Pre – Test level the minimum score at the is 11.61 and the maximum score is 22.07. At the Post – Test level 62.14 is the minimum score and 68.21 is the maximum score.

Table 2: Mean and SD of the Student towards Achievement Score for different Category of Experimental Group

S.No	Variable	Category	Sample Size	Mean		SD	
				Pre-test	Post-Test	Pre-Test	Post-Test
01.	Gender	Boys	21	25.6	81.67	9.66	10.24
		Girls	21	13.81	70.12	7.82	10.62
02.	Caste	OC/BC	26	21.63	76.44	10.56	11.99
		MBC/SC/ST	16	16.56	74.68	9.84	12.58
03.	SMSX	Above 70%	18	18.89	78.89	10.28	9.33
		Below70%	24	19.9	73.65	11.24	13.11
04.	Total		42	19.70	75.89	15.63	11.93

Above table 2 shows that the average Mean Score of the Student towards Achievement Score for different category is 19.70 at Pre – Test level and 75.89 at Post – Test level which show the Eureka Educational Software has considerable effect in Teaching Chemistry. Moreover at the Pre – Test level the minimum score is 13.81 and the maximum score is 25.6. At the Post – Test level 70.12 is the minimum score and 81.67 is the maximum score.

Table 3: Significant Difference between the Mean scores of Control Group and Experimental Group at Pre – Test level

Group	N	Mean	SD	t value	Remarks
Control	37	18.11	11.03	0.661	NS
Experimental	42	19.70	10.58		

NS: Not significant

The above table 3 reveals that the obtained mean Student Achievement Scores in Chemistry of the Control group and Experimental group are more or less same. The calculated 't' value also indicates there is no significant difference at 5% level between Control group and Experimental group at Pre- Test level. Hence the stated Null Hypothesis is that, there is no significant difference between the mean Student Achievement Scores in Chemistry of the Control group and Experimental group at the Pre – Test level is accepted.

Table 4: Significant Difference between the Mean scores of Control Group and Experimental Group at Post – Test level

Group	N	Mean	SD	t value	Remarks
Control	37	64.19	15.63	4.01	S
Experimental	42	75.89	11.93		

S: Significant

It is evident from the table 4 that the obtained mean value of Experimental group is greater than the control group. The calculated 't' value shows that there is significant difference between the Control group and Experimental group. Hence the stated Null hypothesis that there is no significant difference between Student Achievement Scores in Chemistry of Control group and Experimental group at Post – Test level is rejected.

Table 5: Influence of various Category over the performance of the Control Group and Experimental Group at Pre – Test level

Category	Group	N	Mean	SD	t value	Remarks
Boys	Control	18	20.83	9.09	1.59	NS
	Experimental	21	25.6	9.66		
Girls	Control	19	15.53	12.05	0.54	NS
	Experimental	21	13.81	7.82		

OC/BC	Control	23	22.07	11.48	0.14	NS
	Experimental	26	21.63	10.56		
MBC/SC/ST	Control	14	11.61	6.09	1.68	NS
	Experimental	16	16.56	9.84		
Above 70%	Control	21	21.55	10.73	0.78	NS
	Experimental	18	18.89	10.28		
Below 70%	Control	16	13.59	9.72	1.88	NS
	Experimental	24	19.9	11.24		

The above table 5 shows that the calculated 't' values of Control group and Experimental group at the Pre-Test level at various Categories has no significant difference at 5 % level. Hence it is concluded that Gender, Caste, SMSX has no influence over the performance of Control group and Experimental group at the Pre-Test level. Therefore the stated Null hypothesis is that, there is no influence of Gender, Caste, SMSX over the performance of Student Achievement Scores in Chemistry of the Control group and Experimental group at the Pre -Test is accepted.

Table 6: Significant Difference between the Mean scores of Pre-Test and Post-Test for Control Group

Test	N	Mean	SD	t value	Remarks
Pre	37	18.11	11.03	**14.62**	**S**
Post	37	64.19	15.63		

It is evident from the table 6 that the obtained mean value of Post- Test is greater than the Pre-Test. The calculated't' value shows that there is significant difference between the Pre-Test and Post-Test conducted for the Control group. Hence the stated Null hypothesis that there is no significant difference between Student Achievement Scores in Chemistry for the Pre-Test and Post-Test of Control group is rejected.

Table 7: Significant Difference between the Mean scores of Pre-Test and Post-Test for Experimental Group

Test	N	Mean	SD	t value	Remarks
Pre	42	19.70	10.58	**22.61**	**S**
Post	42	75.89	11.93		

The above table 7 reveals that the obtained mean Student Achievement Scores in Chemistry of the Post-Test is greater than Pre-Test of Experimental group. The calculated 't' value also indicates there is significant difference at 5% level between Pre-Test and Post-Test of Experimental group. Hence the stated Null Hypothesis is that, there is no significant difference between the mean Student

Achievement Scores in Chemistry for the Pre-Test and Post-Test of Experimental group is rejected.

Table 8: Influence of Gender over the performance of the Control Group and Experimental Group at Post – Test level

Gender	Group	N	Mean	SD	t value	**Remarks**
Boys	Control	18	65.97	13.31	**4.02**	S
	Experimental	21	81.67	10.24		
Girls	Control	19	62.5	17.37	1.52	NS
	Experimental	21	70.12	10.62		

The above table 8 shows that the calculated 't' values of Control group and Experimental group at the Post -Test level of the Boys has significant difference between the mean scores at 5 % level. The above table also reveals that the calculated 't' values of Control group and Experimental group at the Post-Test level of the Girls has no significant difference between the mean scores at 5 % level. Therefore the stated Null hypothesis is that, except Boys the Girls has no influence over the performance of Student Achievement Scores in Chemistry of the Control group and Experimental group at the Post-Test is accepted.

Table 9: Influence of Caste over the performance of the Control Group and Experimental Group at Post-Test level

Caste	**Group**	**N**	**Mean**	**SD**	**t value**	**Remarks**
OC/BC	Control	23	65.43	16.57	**2.63**	S
	Experimental	26	76.44	11.99		
MBC/SC/ST	Control	14	62.14	13.69	**2.62**	S
	Experimental	16	74.68	12.58		

The calculated 't' values from the above table reveals that Control group and Experimental group at the Post-Test level of the Caste has significant difference between the mean scores at 5 % level. The mean values of the above table shows that there is influence of caste over the performance of Control group and Experimental group at the Post-Test level. Hence the stated Null Hypothesis is that, there is influence of caste over the performance of Student Achievement Scores in Chemistry of the Control group and Experimental group at the Post-Test is rejected.

Table 10: Influence of Students secured Science Marks in Standard X over the performance of the Control Group and Experimental Group at Post-Test level

SMSX	Group	N	Mean	SD	t value	Remarks
Above 70%	Control	21	68.21	11.34	**3.43**	S
	Experimental	18	78.89	9.33		

Below 70%	Control	16	62.66	16.31	**2.45**	S
	Experimental	24	73.65	13.11		

It is evident from the table 10 that the obtained mean value of Experimental group is greater than the Control group. The calculated 't' value shows that there is significant difference between the Control group and Experimental group at the Post- Test level with respect to SMSX at 5 % level. The mean values of the above table shows that there is influence of SMSX over the performance of Control group and Experimental group at the Post-Test level. Hence the stated Null Hypothesis is that, there is influence of SMSX over the performance of Student Achievement Scores in Chemistry of the Control group and Experimental group at the Post-Test is rejected.

FINDINGS & DISCUSSION

The salient findings of the study are i) the Eureka Educational Software has considerable effect in Teaching Chemistry, ii) there is a significant difference between the mean scores of Pre- Test and Post-Test level for both Control Group and Experimental Group, iii) Gender, Caste and SMSX has no influence over the performance of Student Achievement Scores in Chemistry of the Control group and Experimental group at the Pre-Test level, iii) Caste and SMSX has influence over the performance of Student Achievement Scores in Chemistry of the Control group and Experimental group at the Post-Test level and v) Experimental group Boys show significant higher mean scores in the Achievement Scores than the Control group, but Girls has no influence over the performance of Student Achievement Scores in Chemistry of the Control group and Experimental group.

While conducting the Pre-Test it was observed that both Control and Experimental group's posse's similar level of pervious knowledge on the selected contents in Chemistry. The same trend was observed with respect to different variables such as Gender, Caste and SMSX. When the analysis was made between Pre-Test and Post-Test Scores of the Control and Experimental groups it was observed that both methods of teaching such as traditional Lecture Method and Educational Software method, Educational Software method is found to be effective method. While comparing the Mean Achievement Scores between Control and Experimental group it was observed that students who learnt through Eureka Educational Software score significant higher than the Control group Students. The significant difference of the Experimental group may be due to the reason that the Eureka Educational Software has incorporated with interactive presentation, animated movies, special effects and puzzles, these special features might have attracted the Experimental Students to score more marks.

It is interesting to note when comparing the Achievements of Girls Students between Control and Experiment groups the effectiveness was not significant as the Girls Students might not show interest towards Computer Assisted Instruction at XI Standard level.

EDUCATION IMPLICATIONS

This Experimental Study established the positive result on Achievement, so the Educational Institutions may be encouraged to use the Computer Assisted Instruction for the Teaching Learning process. Subject experts may concentrate on preparing Software packages in all the units of the all the subjects and distribute them to Schools. This may make the Students more interest towards Educations and it also make the Teachers to save their time.

CONCLUSIONS

Eureka Educational Software is more suitable method for teaching Chemistry at XI Standard level. Eureka Educational Software is the one of the best method in the Teaching Learning process of Chemistry for XI Standard Students without considering the individual variables such as Gender, Caste and SMSX this is due to the subject contents are taught through more animations and interactions. Due to this Educational Software Students concentrations increased and they easily understood the subject contents. At the Post- Test level the Girls shows no significant difference in the Achievement Scores in Chemistry of the Control group and Experimental group.

REFERENCE

1. Ramesh Chandra (2004). Impact of Media and Technology in Education, Kalpaz Publications, New Delhi.
2. Rao, V.K.(2005). Instructional Technolgy, APH Publishing Corporation, New Delhi.
3. Rawat, S.C. (2004). Essentials of Educational Technology, R.Lall Book Depot, Meerut.
4. Zaidi, S.M. (2004). Educational Technology, Anmol Publisher Pvt. Ltd New Delhi.

❐

7.

An Assessment of Edu Digital Skills among Teachers in Namakkal District

INTRODUCTION

Teacher is an ideal personality whose knowledge and skill play a major role in the development of the nation to the global standard education in general and tapping the potentialities of students to the maximum extent in particular. Teachers are expected to learn forever to withstand the innovations in teaching and updating the knowledge and widen the clarity of the conceptual framework of the subject of specialization too. Unless and until the teachers prepared to meet the requirements and challenges, the dream and purpose of education will not be fulfilled. Nowadays the system of education has assumed the character which involves more students' participation and student centric which is highly enabled through the application of various educational technologies. Edu - digital skills is considered prerequisite for all teachers teaching for nursery to doctorate scholars. 21st century school curriculum has been enriched to meet the demands of world requirements of quality. Communication, collaboration, critical thinking, problem solving, creativity, invention, information and technology literacy and self direction will facilitate the achievement of aims and objectives of education. Teachers of 21st century are expected to equip themselves with modern technology application in teaching and learning process. A paradigm shift has happened to meet the demands of gen y and z learners which require innovative, explorative and interesting approach in teaching and learning. The curriculum will need withstand the futuristic vision for the global scenario. At this juncture the teachers of today should be enthusiastic to update their knowledge and skills forever in order to keep young to the youngest generation whom they meet and it may also be emphasized greatly as the professional ethics. This study has been attempted to assess the knowledge and skills of teachers in the field of information and communication technology which a teacher necessarily possess in the digital world.

EDUCATIONAL DIGITAL SKILLS

It is mentioned that in order to thrive in a digital economy, students will need digital age proficiencies. It is important for the educational system to make parallel changes in order to fulfill its mission in society, namely the preparation of students for the world beyond the classroom. Therefore, the educational system must understand and embrace the following 21st century skills within the context of rigorous academic standards.

The 21st Century Literacy Summit (2002) contends that "the explosive growth of technology in every aspect of society offers us a unique opportunity to engage our citizens in economic and civic life" The report further states that to take advantage of this opportunity, we must continually acquire and develop new knowledge and skills. Summit participants noted "Information and communication technologies are raising the bar on the competencies needed to succeed in the 21st century, and they are compelling us to revisit many of our assumptions and beliefs" The sheer magnitude of human knowledge, world to technology necessitates a shift in our children's education - from plateaus of knowing to continuous cycles of learning. Therefore, policymakers and educators alike must define 21st century skills, highlighting the relationship of those skills to conventional academic standards. As they do so, they must also recognize the need for multiple assessments to measure these skills within the context of academic standards, evaluating their application to today's technological and global society.

TECHNOLOGICAL LITERACY

Demonstrate a sound conceptual understanding of the nature of technology systems and view themselves as proficient users of these systems. Understand and model positive, ethical use of technology in both social and personal contexts. Use a variety of technology tools in effective ways to increase creative productivity. Use communication tools to reach out to the world beyond the classroom and communicate ideas in powerful ways. Use technology effectively to access, evaluate, process and synthesize information from a variety of sources. Use technology to identify and solve complex problems in real-world contexts have been considered as Technological Literacy

INFORMATION LITERACY

Before Accessing Information one should determine what is known and what is needed for problem solving, identify different sources of information, including text, people, video, audio, and databases and prioritize sources based on credibility and relevance. When Accessing Information one need identify and retrieve relevant information from sources and use technology to enhance searching. Revise information-gathering strategies that prove to be in effective when understands how information retrieved does or does not address original problem, evaluate information in terms of credibility and know what are the social, economic, political, legal, and ethical issues that may impact it to facilitate to use technology for evaluation. After Information is extracted, using retrieved information to accomplish a specific purpose, present information clearly and persuasively by using a range of technology tools and media and evaluate the processes and products of these activities have here been considered essential to assure one to be Literate in information.

Global Awareness

Global awareness is knowledge about the connectedness of the nations of the world historically, politically, economically, technologically, socially, linguistically, and ecologically and understand that these interconnections of positive benefits and negative consequences too. The ability to recognize, analyzes, and evaluates major trends in global relations and the interconnections of these trends with both their local and national communities. Participate in the global society by staying current with international news and by participating in the democratic process.

Objectives of the Study

To find the level of Edu-digital skill among school teachers and find whether there is significant different exist among them in relation to their personal variables such as sex, Age, Educational Qualification, Area of Residence, Management of the Institution, Subject of Specialization and the Location of the School.

Research Question

What is the level of educational digital Skills of School Teachers? Is there any Significant Difference Exists among them with respect to their Personal Variables?

Research Methodology

A Normative Descriptive Method of study has been attempted to assess the level of Educational Digital Skills among the School Teachers in Namakkal District

Population, Sample and Sampling Technique of the Study

All teachers who teach in school education are the population of the study and the sample of the study has been chosen from teachers work in Namakkal district only and the sample was taken by stratified random sampling technique which consists of 250.

Tools and Technique of Data Collection

A tool consisted of 24 items related to some basic skills necessary for adopting computer enabled teaching technology, using internet connection which will benefit students to gain knowledge, understand the concept better, improve the critical thinking, problem solving ability, creativity and to enhance their communication skill and appropriate application of the knowledge gained for the betterment of himself and to the society. The scope of this study extent all teachers who teach in the classroom from kindergarten to plus two levels. The questionnaire has dimensions of using the computer for retrieving useful information via internet, knowledge about various search engines, and preparation of effective PowerPoint materials, video clippings, software package application, audio recording, connecting to virtual classroom and the facilities to publish the students works in internet. Knowledge and the application of MS word, Excel format, mobile for teaching and learning purpose and the ability to set ready LCD, mike and arrange show in the smart classroom and the application of social media in education have also been taken for assessing.

Scoring Procedure & Statistical Tools Used

The Questionnaire used in the study has five point scale of the level of skill of the respondents in relation to their digital skill hence it has five options of known very well, known, moderately known, known little and Unknown which scored as 5, 4,3,2 and 1 respectively.

SPSS package has been used to analyze the data and the percentage analysis and the differential analysis have been used to describe and infer the details pertaining to the research question formulated for the study.

Table 1: An Analysis of Edu Digital Skills among Teachers in Namakkal District

Items	Very well Known		Well Known		Moderately Known		Known Little		Unknown		Total
	F	%	F	%	F	%	F	%	F	%	
Information Retrieval	41	16.4	59	23.6	62	24.8	75	30	13	5.2	250
Power point preparation	52	20.8	67	26.8	53	21.2	60	24	18	7.2	250
Efficient use of Windows operating system	35	14	48	19.2	75	30	81	32.4	11	4.4	250
Connecting to the Online Teaching of World Classroom	15	6	20	8	39	15.6	116	46.4	60	24	250
Skill in make it work well of LCD mike screen view	15	6	26	10.4	77	30.8	114	45.6	18	7.2	250

Items	Very well Known		Well Known		Moderately Known		Known Little		Unknown		Total
Knowledge about E learning material preparation	21	8.4	15	6	27	10.8	129	51.6	58	23.2	250
Account in social networking sites like Face-book, twitter	22	8.8	36	14.4	74	29.6	12	4.8	106	42.4	250
Using of videos and computer games in teaching	19	7.6	29	11.6	55	22	85	34	62	24.8	250
Application of Virtual classrooms and chat rooms in teaching and learning	13	5.2	18	7.2	17	6.8	56	22.4	146	58.4	250
Application of documentary film in deliverance of the instructional objectives	51	20.4	60	24	41	16.4	31	12.4	67	26.8	250
Using of web-Camera in virtual interaction	16	6.4	41	16.4	27	10.8	71	28.4	95	38	250
Application of white Board in teaching	25	10	16	6.4	19	7.6	43	17.2	147	58.8	250
Safety and security issues in using webmail	17	6.8	39	15.6	90	36	70	28	44	17.6	250
Security Challenges in instant messaging	15	6	35	14	78	31.2	98	39.2	24	9.6	250
Application of iPod and tables in teaching	11	4.4	23	9.2	67	26.8	80	32	69	27.6	250
Application of Video conferencing for teaching and learning	32	12.8	24	9.6	71	28.4	90	36	33	13.2	250
Application of YouTube	49	19.6	86	34.4	55	22	62	24.8	38	15.2	250

Items	Very well Known		Well Known		Moderately Known		Known Little		Unknown		Total
Application of Flicker & Picasa	19	7.6	25	10	62	24.8	104	41.6	40	16	250
Application of mobile phone for transferring data of video	21	8.4	27	10.8	80	32	90	36	32	12.8	250
Application of mobile phone for transferring data of voice	22	8.8	33	13.2	76	30.4	81	32.4	38	15.2	250
Application of mobile phone for transferring data of text	187	74.8	46	18.4	3	1.2	9	3.6	5	2	250
Assessment of students performance through online	25	10	52	20.8	58	23.2	105	42	10	4	250
Application of learning Management System - LMS	11	4.4	21	8.4	37	14.8	57	22.8	15	6	250
Application of Video-recording	17	6.8	26	10.4	51	20.4	78	31.2	78	31.2	250

Majority of teachers have necessary in Skill and knowledge in the application of MS office, Mobile technology in teaching and learning, information retrieval system from online resource centre but the majority teachers have moderate and least knowledge about e-content preparation, application of social media, and security issues in web mails, various learning management system and efficient use of ICT in teaching

Table 2: Significance of Difference in Edu-Digital Skill of Teachers

Demographic Variables	P Value	Level of Sig.
Sex	0.153	NS
Area of Residence	0.104	NS
Location of the School	0.214	NS
Teaching Experience	0.098	NS

Educational Qualification	0.521	NS
Management of the School	0.021*	S
Subject of Specialization	0.001**	S

There is no significant difference exist among the respondents in their Educational digital skill in relation to their personal variables of Sex, Area of Residence, Location of the School, Teaching Experience and their educational qualification. But the statistical report of analysis shows that there is significant difference exist among the sample in relation to their management of the school and their subject of specialization.

Educational Implications

1. Teacher Education curriculum should emphasize the ICT enabled education in B.Ed program
2. Workshops need to be conducted for B.Ed program in the practical application of ICT and training program can be organized for E- content preparation
3. Orientation and Refresher courses for the teachers in schools should be conducted frequently to enable teachers to facilitate them in the efficient use of ICT in teaching and learning environment
4. Collaborative Approach should be made in integrating ICT in education

Conclusion

Teachers are the forerunner of all developments and growth of the nation and the world; they play a significant role in bringing desirable outcome in the world with their adaptability and their ever learning behavior of updating knowledge and skills in any field. No technology can replace the teacher in any period of time but the teacher needs possess skills in the application of technology which facilitate desirable educational outcome in the field of education.

References

1. Felix.A & Jahitha Begum (2011) "An Awareness of E-resources related to ICT and Educaation among M.Ed Students and M.Phil Scholars" ICT in teaching and learning, APH Publishing Corporation, New Delhi, p.169
2. Nagarajan .K (2009) "Educational Innovations and Management" Ram Publishers, Chennai. Pp.135-185.
3. Natchimuthu.K (2012), "Need of E-Content Development in Education Today" APH Publication Corporation, New Delhi. P.76.
4. Rangarajan. P & Senthilnathan.S (2012) "Teacher Educators Attitude towards E Learning" Edutracks, Vol.No.12 No.1 pp. 21-32.

❐

8.

Effectiveness of Multimedia Programme in Perceiving Human Anatomy among Higher Secondary Students

INTRODUCTION

In view of growing importance of science education, old concepts of science teaching have therefore, rather become completely outmoded and an entirely new ethos and approach to science curriculum have come into existence. Moreover, unprecedented development of scientific research, new discoveries, and new methods of investigation, in the early twentieth century, has created a need and urge to examine and reorganize science teaching programmes at all levels in schools. Institutions are functioning in an era of rapidly emerging new technologies. Some of them, like information and communications technology, have fuelled a veritable explosion of rising expectations everywhere. When such is the pace of developmental processes, it becomes fairly imperative on the part of the students not only to possess sound knowledge and understanding of fundamental concepts, but also to understand and appreciate the ramifications of various developments in the field of science and technology, especially in the context of their future career. The situation underscores the significance of research in science education and it is time for the educationists to evolve a proper and appropriate strategy for teaching science.

At the Higher Secondary level, the science subject is divided into Physics, Chemistry, Botany, and Zóology according to Tamil Nadu State Board syllabus. Zoology deals with the life history, distribution, structure, reproduction, and importance of animals including Homosapiens, the human beings. 'Human anatomy' is one of the units of the Zoology subject. Human anatomy is the branch of anatomy devoted to the structure of the human body. In general the study of human anatomy helps the students to do their higher studies in Medicine, Physiotherapy, Nursing, Degree courses like B.Sc., Zoology, and Microbiology etc. Apart from acquiring the technical knowledge, it is necessary for human beings to know and control their own systems of their body for healthy life. Hence the investigator has selected the unit "human anatomy" to teach through multimedia programme for the higher secondary students in the present investigation.

An instructional or teaching strategy refers to a pattern of teaching act that serves to attain certain goals and to guard against others. An instructional strategy is a purposefully-conceived and determined plan of action. It also occupies a central position in formal education. Instructional strategies aim at establishing relationship between teaching inputs and learning outputs, mainly in terms of realizing the learning outcomes. Instructional strategies include teaching methods, approaches and techniques.

Methods of instruction may be teacher-centered such as Historical method, Biographical method, Lecture method, Lecture-demonstration method or pupil-centered method which includes group methods such as project method, discussion, seminar and workshop. The pupil-centered methods also include individual methods such as programmed instruction, Computer Aided Instruction, Instructional Modules and Multimedia packages.

REVIEW OF LITERATURE

Chang, Kuo-En et al. (2008) studied **the effects of learning support in simulation-based physics learning.** The results of the study revealed that the outcome for learning about the basic characteristics of an optical lens was significantly better for simulation-based learning than for laboratory learning.

Djeassilane (2008) investigated the effect of computer aided instruction (CAI) in enhancing the academic achievement of higher secondary students in commerce. The findings of the study showed that the computer aided instruction was effective in helping the students of the experimental group to perform better in the post-test. It proved the effectiveness of the computer aided instruction in commerce developed by the investigator. And also it was found that the experimental students had more favourable attitude towards computer assisted instruction.

Garnett, Hackling and Oliver (2009) developed an interactive multimedia package to improve students' understanding of the particulate basis of chemical reaction, and their ability to interpret chemical equations and solve problems based on equations. The study showed that Interactive multimedia provided learners with access to a rich information source and appropriate activities to promote learning and understanding.

Junaidu, Sahalu (2009) studied effectiveness of multimedia in learning & teaching data structures online. This paper explores and reports on the importance of creating multimedia-rich course content and the important role that animations can play in creating a successful online learning experience. Results indicated that students consistently perform much better in questions requiring application of material taught in carefully animated algorithms. These results should carry over to other educational environments.

Liao, Yuen-kuang C., Chang, Huei-wen and Chen, Yu-wen (2009) compared the effects of computer applications (i.e., computer-assisted instruction, computer simulations, and Web-based learning) versus traditional instruction on elementary school students' achievement in Taiwan. The results suggest that computer application instruction is more effective than traditional instruction for elementary school students in Taiwan.

O'Day, Danton (2010) studied on "using animations to teach biology: past & future research on the attributes that underlie pedagogically sound animations". Multiple technical resources (commonly referred to as multimedia) are currently used by many instructors to communicate difficult topics and concepts to their students in meaningful ways. Various sources have shown that animations are more effective than static sequential images. This study evaluated how animations can be and have been used as effective teaching and learning tools in biology and what more needs to be done to understand their true value.

Ozmen, Haluk (2010) studied on "The influence of CAI on students' conceptual understanding of chemical Bonding and attitude towards chemistry: A case for Turkey". The results of this study suggested that teaching-learning of topics in chemistry related to chemical bonding can be improved by the use of computer-assisted teaching materials.

Ponraj and Nellaiyapen (2010) investigated the effectiveness of CAI in teaching Zoology. The major finding of the study showed that the experimental group performed better than the Control group in the post-test. The results of the study revealed that experimental method of teaching is more effective than the traditional method of teaching the topic 'Nucleus' in Zoology.

Pryor, Caroline and Bitter, Gary (2010) used multimedia to teach in-service teachers and studied its impacts on learning, application, and retention. The study found that the video modeling in the module was effective in helping teachers learn, and discourse strategies were learned, applied, and retained.

Rotbain, Marbach-Ad and Stavy (2011) used a computer animation to teach high school molecular biology. The achievements of the experimental group were compared with those of a control group. Analysis of the post-test showed that the mean score of the experimental group was significantly higher than the mean score of the control group.

Venkataraman (2011) prepared software packages (CAI) for XI standard physics and studied the effectiveness of its among selected modes of CAI in physics in relation to learners' personality. The results of the study showed that the CAI is effective with different modes. Computer Assisted Instruction shows significant difference in the achievement of different instructional objectives. Further Computer Assisted Instruction enhances the retention of the learnt content.

Vernadakis et al. (2012) examined the effect of multimedia computer-assisted instruction (MCAI), traditional instruction (TI), and combined instruction (CI) methods on learning the skill of shooting in basketball. Additionally, a comparison of the students' attitudes towards the MCAI and TI methods was made. Students took pre-, post-, and retention written test covering techniques and rules of the games. Post-test results indicated no significant differences between the groups concerning the written test. Nevertheless, the attitude test scores of the CI group were more favourable to MCAI method than the TI method. Retention test results showed that groups retained the knowledge acquisition. However, the combined method of instruction tended to be the most effective for cognitive learning.

Victor, Adeosun Olufemi (2012) investigated the relative effects of three multi-media instructional packages on Nigerian students' achievement in social studies. The purpose was to determine which of the combinations of videotape recording presentation, pictures and the chalk and talk method; the combination of audiotape recording presentation, pictures and the chalk and talk method and the combination of pictures and the chalk and talk method. The study revealed that the combination of pictures and the chalk and talk method was most effective among the packages tested in the learning of social studies.

OBJECTIVES

1. To develop a Multimedia Programme for the unit of Human anatomy from XI standard Zoology subject in order to teach the higher secondary students.
2. To find out the effectiveness of Multimedia Programme in teaching Human anatomy among higher secondary students.

METHODOLOGY

The methodology adopted for the study is explained in detail. The sampling technique, size of the sample, variables of the study, description of the tool used and administration of tool are elaborated.

Sample

A samples of 100 higher secondary students in selected randomly were studied in Tindivanam Town.

Data Collection

The present study aims at developing and using Multimedia programme for perceiving human anatomy for higher secondary students to enable them to understand the concepts very easily through individualized instructional technique. It is maintained that the Multimedia programme may reduce monotony in the classroom by bringing out real life situations and motivate them for self-study and provides opportunities for individual pace and ability.

The study intends to develop a multimedia programme for human anatomy for XI standard Zoology subject prescribed by Tamil Nadu State Board Syllabus and find out the effectiveness of the Multimedia programme through experimentation in perceiving human anatomy among the higher secondary students. The study provides scope for the development and use of many Multimedia programmes in the concerned discipline as well as other disciplines for the benefit of learners of different categories. Hence the multimedia programme can be used as an individualized instructional technique for the students of different categories in the science subjects as well as other subjects.

ANALYSIS AND INTERPRETATION

Performance of control group students between the pre test and post test in human anatomy.

The Mean, Standard Deviation and Co-efficient of Variation were computed for the control group students in their performance in human anatomy between the pre test and post test.

Table 1: Distribution of Mean, Standard Deviation and Co-efficient of Variation on the performance of control group students between the pre test and post test in human anatomy

Group	N	Mean	S.D	CV
Pre test	100	42.69	13.60	31.86
Post test	100	52.46	13.28	25.31

The Co-efficient of Variation of the pre test and post test for the control group students was found to be 31.86 and 25.31, which reveals that the control group students are more consistent in their performance in human anatomy in the post test than the pre test. It reveals that the control group students have improved in their performance in human anatomy in the post test than the pre test.

To find out the significance of the difference between the control and experimental group students in their performance in human anatomy in the pre test, the 't' test was used.

Table 2: Distribution of 't' value between the control and experimental group students in their performance in human anatomy in the pre test

Group	N	Mean	S.D	't' value	Level of Significant
Control	100	42.69	13.60	0.17	p>0.05
Experimental	100	43.31	12.59		

There is no significant difference between the control and experimental group students in their performance in human anatomy in the pre test.

The obtained 't' value 0.17 is not statistically significant since it is less than the table 't' value 1.96 for 50 df at 0.05 level of significance. Hence the null hypothesis is accepted. It shows that there is no significant difference between the control and experimental group students in their performance in human anatomy in the pre test. It is therefore concluded that both control and experimental group students have the same level of performance in human anatomy in the pre test.

To find out the significance of the difference between the control and experimental group students in their performance in human anatomy in the post test, the 't' test was used.

Table 3: Distribution of 't' value between the control and experimental group students in their performance in human anatomy in the post test

Group	N	Mean	S.D	't' value	Level of Significant
Control	100	52.46	13.28	14.38	p<0.05
Experimental	100	92.81	5.31		

There is no significant difference between the control and experimental group students in their performance in human anatomy in the post test.

The obtained 't' value 14.38 is statistically significant since it is greater than the table 't' value 1.96 for 50 df at 0.05 level of significance. Hence the null hypothesis is rejected. It shows that there is significant difference between the control and experimental group students in their performance in human anatomy in the post test. It is therefore concluded that the experimental group students performed significantly better in human anatomy than that of control group students in the post test.

Table 4: Distribution of 't' value for the pre and post test mean scores of control group students in the performance in human anatomy

Group	N	Mean	S.D	't' value	Level of Significant
Pre test	100	42.69	13.60	2.62	p<0.05
Post test	100	52.46	13.28		

There is no significant difference between the pre and post test mean scores of control group students in the performance in human anatomy.

The obtained 't' value 2.62 is statistically significant since it is greater than the table 't' value 1.96 for 50 df at 0.05 level of significance. Hence the null hypothesis is rejected. It shows that there is significant difference between the pre and post test mean scores of control group students in the performance in human anatomy. It is therefore concluded that the control group students have improved in their performance in human anatomy in the post test.

SUGGESTIONS

The present study aims at developing and using Multimedia programme for perceiving human anatomy for higher secondary students to enable them to understand the concepts very easily through individualized instructional technique. It is maintained that the Multimedia programme may reduce monotony in the classroom by bringing out real life situations and motivate them for self-study and provides opportunities for individual pace and ability.

CONCLUSION

The study intends to develop a multimedia programme for human anatomy for XI standard Zoology subject prescribed by Tamil Nadu State Board Syllabus and find out the effectiveness of the Multimedia programme through experimentation in perceiving human anatomy among the higher secondary students. The study provides scope for the development and use of many Multimedia programmes in the concerned discipline as well as other disciplines for the benefit of learners of different categories. Hence the multimedia programme can be used as an individualized instructional technique for the students of different categories in the science subjects as well as other subjects. The present study reveals that the experiment group students who used multimedia programme performed significantly better than that of the control group students who did not use, which implies that the multimedia programme has tremendous impact upon the performance in human anatomy than the students learning through traditional method. This proves the effectiveness of the multimedia programme in human anatomy developed by the investigator. The present study reveals that the performance of the control and experimental group students in the post test is significantly higher than the pre test. But the performance of the experimental group students in the post test is more significantly higher than the post test performance of control group students. Thus, it proves the supremacy of the multimedia programme over traditional method.

REFERENCES

1. Chang, Kuo-En; Chen, Yu-Lung; Lin, He-Yan; Sung, Yao-Ting (2008). Effects of learning support in simulation-based physics learning. Computers & Education, 51(4): 1486-1498..

2. Djeassilane, N. (2008). Effect of computer aided instruction (CAI) in enhancing the academic achievement of higher secondary students in commerce. Unpublished Doctoral Dissertation, Alagappa University, Karaikudi.
3. Garnett, P., Hackling, M., & Oliver, R. (2009). Designing interactive multimedia materials to support concept development in beginning chemistry classes.
4. Junaidu, Sahalu (2009). Effectiveness of multimedia in learning & teaching data structures online. Turkish Online Journal of Distance Education-TOJDE,9(4),Article 7.Retrieved March.
5. Liao, Yuen-kuang C., Chang, Huei-wen & Chen, Yu-wen (2009). Effects of Computer Applications on Elementary School Students' Achievement: A Meta-Analysis of Students in Taiwan. Computers in the Schools, 24(3-4): 43-64. Retrieved.
6. O'Day, Danton H. (2010). Using animations to teach biology: past & future research on the attributes that underlie pedagogically sound animations. The American Biology Teacher, 70(5):274-278. Retrieved March 20.
7. Ozmen, Haluk (2010). The influence of Computer-Assisted Instruction on students' conceptual understanding of chemical Bonding and Attitude toward chemistry: A case for Turkey. Computers and Education, 51(1): 423-438. Retrieved March.
8. Ponraj, P., & Nellaiyapen, N. O. (2010). CAI in teaching Zoology. Research and Reflections on Education, 6(2): 18-21.
9. Pryor, Caroline R., & Bitter, Gary G. (2010). Using multimedia to teach in-service teachers: Impacts on learning, application, and retention. Computers in Human Behavior, 24 (6): 2668-2681. Retrieved March.
10. Rotbain, Y., Marbach-Ad, G., & Stavy, R. (2011). Using a computer animation to teach high school molecular biology. Journal of Science Education and Technology, 17(1): 49 – 58. Retrieved March.
11. Venkataraman, S. (2011). Relative effectiveness among selected modes of CAI in physics in relation to learner's personality. Unpublished Doctoral Dissertation, Annamalai University. Chidambaram.
12. Vernadakis, N., Zetou, E., Tsitskari, E., Giannousi, M., & Kioumourtzoglou, E. (2012). Student attitude and learning outcomes of multimedia computer-assisted versus traditional instruction in basketball. Education and Information Technologies, 13(3): 167-183.
13. Victor, Adeosun Olufemi (2012). Relative effects of three Multi-Media Instructional Packages on Nigerian student's achievement in Social Studies. Pakistan Journal of Social Sciences, 5 (5): 415 – 420. Retrieved March.

❐

9.

Students Attitude towards Audio-Visual Aids Used By the Teachers

INTRODUCTION

Audio Visual aids or Graphic aids are the form of visuals that are represented on plane surface. The subject matter areas that are represented in Audio Visual aids or Graphic aids are in an abridged and easily understandable form. They convey meaning mainly through relatively conventionalized symbols that are nearer to reality perceptually than verbal symbols. They secure the attention of the pupils by their attractive format and simplicity of layout. They convey the expected message by combination of visual and pictorial message made meaningful by suitable captions. Pictures and words blended in harmony deliver the required information. The idea conveyed by any graphic aid should be a single concept. The layout and words should not be complicated so as to puzzle the viewer and make him lose interest in the same. The statement "one good visual which can secure and maintain attention and educate the viewer in the desired area is worth a thousand words" is quite correct. Graphics could be truly considered as the shorthand language of the idea presented. The criteria for good graphics are that they should be simple, bold, legible, brief and have adequate margins. Graphics are only two-dimensional and should be carefully planned to offset the limitation. An Audio Visual aids or a graphic aid by eliminating non–essentials and by using bold symbolic representations with attractive portrayal should be able to create interest and secure the attention of the pupils. Since the message to be conveyed pertains to a single concept and hence brief, the viewer will not get perplexed on being exposed to the visual but will try to read and understand what is implied (visual and words).Audio Visual aids or a graphic aids could easily be prepared by and teacher using simple materials that are easily available and stored for future use. Making graphics should form an integral part of the teacher's preparation for teaching. Almost any material involving illustrations is basically graphic in nature. There can be an infinite variety of graphic materials. It is difficult to give a rigid list of these materials. The present study aims to find out the students attitude towards audio-visual aids used by the teachers in Coimbatore district. A samples of 100 respondents selected randomly were studied. An interview schedule method of survey was used to find out the attitude towards audio-visual aids. Primary data were collected by using a structured interview scheduled. All the respondents were asked the same questions in the same fashion and they were informed the purpose of study. ANOVA, t-test and regression analysis were applied to test the hypotheses. The data collected through questionnaires have been tabulated. The findings and observations are the result and outcome of the interpretations made during the study of analysis.

Graphs, Diagram, Posters, Maps, Comics, Cartoons, Charts, Globes, Display Board, Peg Boards, Hook and loop board, felt board, magnetic board, marker board, chalk board, bulletin board, models, Epidiascope, slight projector, over head projector (OHP), fields trips, excursion, exhibition, museums, radio, Television, Tape recorder, Video Caste Record VCR and Computers. By using audio visual materials in accessible process, materials givens objects changes in time, speed and space could easily be brought to the class. Audio visual aids can helps to imaginative teachers to solve the communication problems. It also helps to extend human experience. Use of audio visual aids results in greater acquisition of knowledge of facts and ensures longer retention of the information gained. It can provide effective substitutes for direct contact of students with environment-social and physical. It also adds an expected change in attitude and behaviour of the students. It can provide integrated experiences varying from abstract to concrete. It helps in to secure and retain to attention as well as develop the communication skills. It could be used to motivate and stimulate interest of students to gain further knowledge. Lastly, In a conventional teaching method teacher is the centre of attention and the primary sources of information.

An attitude is a mental state of readiness exerting directive or dynamic influence upon individual's response to all objects and situations with which it is related. Therefore if we can have some judgement about the attitude of an individual towards a specific thing or activity then we can have a fair idea as to whether the individual can be persuaded to participate in a particular thing or activity and whether he shall adopt it with interest and sincerity or not.

The attitude is the degree of positive or negative effect associated with some psychological objects namely institution, ideal, symbol, phrase, slogan, job or idea towards which people can differ with respect to positive or negative effect (Thurstone, 1946). The attitude is a dispositional readiness to respond to certain situations, persons, objects in a consistent manner which has been learnt and has become one's typical mode of response (Free Mann, 1950). According to Guild

(1950) attitude is a tendency of individual to favour or not to favour some type of situation. The attitude may be considered as motivational perceptual states, which direct perceptions and predispose a person to act in accordance with perceptions (Allport, 1955). The attitudes are learnt pre-dispositions to respond positively to certain objects, situations, institutions, concepts or other persons (Aiken, 1979).

REVIEW OF LITERATURE

Glee Harrah Cady and **Pat Mc Gregor (2005**) describes that "Internet is a network of network and the internet mostly connects network of computers".

Barry (2006) studied the relationship between student's perceptions of their science class room learning environment and attitude to four different scores of scientific information experiments, books, promote positive attitude towards experiment as a source of information, while less favorable environment promoted more positive attitude to the more authoritarian sources of information.

Schafer (2007) compared third and fourth grade students using ESS units with students using laid low science serious on classification skills, science achievements and science attitudes. No achievement or classification skill different were noted but ESS students had more favorable attitudes.

Williams (2008), "Attitude of high school pupils towards general science and its relationship with achievement and its subjects". In her study it is found to examine if there are any differences among the different groups of students such as boys and girls. Rural school pupil and Urban school pupils in respect of their achievement in science, attitude towards science and attitude forwards science education.

Martis Anandi (2009) developed the test on scientific attitudes (TOSA), taking the point of view that attitudes must be inferred from the behavior of students. They developed a multiple – choice format test. The developed behavioral definitions of eight attitudes: (1) critical mindedness, (2) suspended judgment (3) Respect for evidence (4) Honesty, (5) Objectivity, (6) Willingness to change opinions, (7) Open – mindedness and (8) Questioning attitude. The behavioral definitions to these eight attitudes were used to develop items.

Mohanty Ajay Kumar (2010) investigated attitudes towards education, critical thinking ability and specific effective behavious of (1) Students who had studied, the BSCS environmental models "Investing your Environment" (IYE), (2) Those students using one of BSCS biological science version and (3) Those studying models of Biology. He found that the ability of students who had experienced BSCS Biological science was significantly increased but no other differences were found among the students on any of the other variables.

OBJECTIVES

The present study attempts to investigate the attitude towards Audio-visual aids used by the teachers.

METHODOLOGY

Methodology is an important aspect of any research work. There are different methods followed at various stages of any investigation. The details of methods followed in this study such as selection of tools, sample frame, collection of data, and analysis of data are involved in this research paper. The study has been designed with the student's attitude towards Audio-visual aids used by the teacher's achievement. The major aim of the present study is to determine the student's Audio-visual aids used by the teacher.

Method of data collection

The investigator personally distributed the questionnaires to each member of the randomly selected sample. They were requested to answer the items in the booklet as per the instructions provided at the beginning of each questionnaire. Confidentiality of response was assured. The questionnaires were collected by the investigator from the employees. The responses were scored as per the scoring key of the respective questionnaire. Then the results were tabulated, analysed and discussed.

Sample

A sample is a finite number of observations (or) cases in a particular universe of which it is a pat (Good 1952). The investigator prepared a representative random sample of students studying VIII & IX standard in different schools at Coimbatore District. A sample of 100 students was finally selected

HYPOTHESIS

Students have favorable attitude towards use of Audio Visual Aids in Coimbatore district school.

Nature of the Tool

The inventory contained general instruction for the students and information about bio data. In addition to that the specific instruction ware given to on the first page of the inventory. Space for collecting personal data like students name type of school, locality of the school, class, gender, community, religion, group, medium of instruction, birth order of the child and parental literacy.

Data Processing

The collected data were analysed using appropriate statistical techniques. The descriptive statistics such as mean and S.D, t-ratio were computed. In order to study the functional dependencies to indicate the likelihood of causal relationships between the variables, inferential statistical techniques of ANOVA and Percentage analysis were computed.

ANALYSIS AND INTERPRETATION

Table 1: Showing Mean, SD and t-test for respondent about students attitude towards audio visual aids used by the teachers on the basis of type of the school.

Types of the school	N	Mean	SD	t-value	LS
Government	62	70.48	6.50	2.78	0.01
Private	38	73.30	10.33		

Hypothesis 1: Students do not differ in their student's attitude towards audio visual aids used by the teachers on the basis of types of the school.

The calculated t-value (2.78), which is significant at 0.01 level, confirms that there is a significant difference in student audio visual aids on the basis of type of the school. Hence the stated hypothesis is rejected. So government students have high level of audio visual aids than private school students.

Table 2: Showing Mean, SD and t-test for respondent about students attitude towards audio visual aids used by the teachers on the basis of locality of the school.

Locality of the school	N	Mean	SD	t-value	LS
Urban	74	72.24	8.11	1.07	NS
Rural	26	71.14	9.19		

Hypothesis 2: Students do not differ in their student's attitude towards audio visual aids used by the teachers on the basis of locality of the school.

The calculated t-value (1.07), which is not significant at 0.05 level, confirms that there is no significant difference in their audio visual aids on the basis of locality of the school. Hence the stated hypothesis is accepted.

Table 3: Showing Mean, SD and t-test for respondent about students attitude towards audio visual aids used by the teachers on the basis of Gender.

Gender	N	Mean	SD	t-value	LS
Male	74	70.97	7.41	1.85	NS
Female	26	72.90	9.89		

Hypothesis 3: Students do not differ in their student's attitude towards audio visual aids used by the teachers on the basis of gender.

The calculated t-value (1.85), which is not significant at 0.05 level, confirms that there is no significant difference in their audio visual aids on the basis of gender. Hence the stated hypothesis is accepted.

Table 4: Showing Mean, SD and t-test for respondent about students attitude towards audio visual aids used by the teachers on the basis of group.

Group	N	Mean	SD	t-value	LS
Arts	56	69.19	5.37	5.58	0.01
Science	44	74.58	10.37		

Hypothesis 4: Students do not differ in their attitude towards audio visual aids used by the teachers on the basis of group.

The calculated t-value (5.58), which is significant at 0.01 level, confirms that there is a significant difference in student audio visual aids on the basis of group. Hence the stated hypothesis is rejected. So science students have high level of audio visual aids than art students.

Table 5: Showing Mean, SD and F-ratio for students attitude towards audio visual aids used by the teachers on the basis of medium of instruction.

Medium of instruction	N	Mean	SD	F-ratio	LS
Hindi	50	70.20	9.64	6.49	0.01
English	30	71.75	4.19		
Kannada	20	75.00	11.60		
Total	100	71.78	8.58		

Hypothesis 5: Students do not differ in their attitude towards audio visual aids used by the teachers on the basis of medium of instruction.

The calculated F-ratio (6.49), which is not significant at 0.05 level, confirms that there is a significant difference in students attitude of audio visual aids on the basis of medium of instruction. Hence the stated hypothesis is rejected.

Table 6: Regression for student demographic characters and their attitude towards audio visual aids used by the teachers.

MODEL SUMMARY

Model	R	R Square	Adjusted R Square	Std. Error of the Estimate
1	.436[a]	.190	.159	7.87

a. Predictors: (Constant)

ANOVA[B]

Model	Sum of Squares	df	Mean Square	F	Sig.
Regression	.4189.756	11	380.887	6.155	.000[a]
Residual	17821.724	88	61.881		
Total	22011.480	99			

a. Predictors: (Constant)
b. Dependent variable

COEFFICIENTS[A]

Model	Unstandardized Coefficients		Standardized Coefficients	t	Sig.
	B	Std. Error	Beta		
Name of the school	58.979	4.376		13.477	.000
Type of the school	2.387	1.116	.139	2.139	.033**
Locality of the school	-1.000	1.005	-.058	-.995	.320
Class	-.500	1.046	-.028	-.478	.633
Gender	1.989	1.052	.115	1.891	.060
Community	-1.365	.422	-.190	-3.233	.001**
Religion	.757	.627	.068	1.208	.228
Groups	5.255	.947	.306	5.548	.000**
Medium of instruction	2.183	.649	.191	3.365	.001**
Birth order of the child	-9.11	1.032	-.001	-.009	.993
Parental literacy (Father)	-.143	1.003	-.008	-.143	.887
Parental literacy (Mother)	-.585	.955	-.033	-.612	.541

a. Dependent Variable: Attitude towards Audi visual aids

** Significant at 0.01 level

According to the regression result it is known that the demographic variables are influenced nearly 19 per cent to measure their attitude towards audio visual aids. This is proved by the obtained r square value (0.19).

Further the calculated F-value (6.15) also significant at 0.01 level. It indicates that there is a significant influence between students demographic characters and their attitude towards audio visual aids.

Also from the obtained t- values the demographic variables such as type of school, community, group studied and medium of instructions the students studied are significant at 0.01 level. So it is concluded that there is a significant difference regarding attitude towards audio visual aids on the basis of these variables.

CONCLUSION

Audio Visual aids or graphic aids are the form of visuals that are represented on plane surface. The subject – matter areas that are represented in Audio Visual aids or graphic aids are in an abridged and easily understandable form. They convey meaning mainly through relatively conventionalized symbols that are nearer to reality perceptually than verbal symbols. They secure the attention of the pupils by their attractive format and simplicity of layout. They convey the expected message by combination of visual and pictorial message made meaningful by suitable captions. Pictures and words blended in harmony deliver the required information.

The idea conveyed by any graphic aid should be a single concept. The layout and words should not be complicated so as to puzzle the viewer and make him lose interest in the same. The statement "one good visual which can secure and maintain attention and educate the viewer in the desired area is worth a thousand words" is quite correct. Graphics could be truly considered as the shorthand language of the idea presented. The criteria for good graphics are that they should be simple, bold, legible, brief and have adequate margins.

Findings of the study

- Based on the results that students do not differ in their audio visual aids on the basis of types of the school.
- From the calculation that students do not differ in their audio visual aids on the basis of locality of the school.
- Based on the results that students do not differ in their audio visual aids on the basis of gender.
- Based on the results that students do not differ in their audio visual aids on the basis of group.
- From the analysis that students do not differ in their audio visual aids on the basis of medium of instruction.

DISCUSSION

Audio visual aids a process of inward journey to unravel the hidden potentialities of a being. It helps an individual to develop ones personality. A systematic approach of Audio visual aids helps an individual to see the all around development at physical, mental, intellectual and emotional level. The practice of use of audio visual aids makes an individual perfect. It removes the unwanted elements in the mind of the learner. It improves concentration and brings mental stability. Audio visual aids is an essential tool for students to achieve higher score in their studies as if improve concentration, memory and skills. The present study clearly indicates and recommends the students to use of audio visual aids as to develop positive attitude towards everything in their life which helps to excel themselves in their studies. The entire study concluded reveals that the use of audio visual aids has high achievement and expressed more favourable attitude.

Educational Implications

Audio-visual aids are very important and useful aids for teaching. As well as it creates high interest among the students to learn the subjects. So, the department of education shall take a step to implement the latest audio-visual aids to all the school and colleges for teaching purpose.

For self-learning, these types of aids are very helpful to the students. Also students are very much interested in using latest technologies such as computers and internet. In internet lot of facilities are there to learn new information with visual appearance. From that students are also get more interest to use that.

In the case of teaching, in older days teachers follow interactive methods and oral demonstration. But these are not creating much interest. In order to create interest and attention audio-visual aids are highly useful. So, the concerned educational institution tries to provide these facilities. So that teachers and students get benefited.

Suggestions

The following suggestions are arrived from the research findings. Research found that use of audio visual aids will contribute more in students achievement. Also the result reveals that use of audio visual aids increases the memory power, concentration. Further it sharpens the intelligence. Apart from that it reduces misconception in learning. Further due to use of audio visual aids the sensory expression would be more exercised. So, the present research suggested that in all schools and colleges, the students advised to use of audio visual aids compulsory. The education department forms a rule for that and advises the educational institutions make a step to establish separate infrastructure for this one. Also the Government take a step to use audio visual aids effectively students in their academic. This will definitely help the students to be a good learner imbibing the concepts.

Conclusion

The present study attempted to identify the students attitude towards audio-visual aids used by the teachers. For that the researcher framed some objectives. On the basis of objectives, a questionnaire is framed. After framing the questionnaire, these are circulated to the selected samples. 100 samples were selected randomly. The responses were collected and coded using computerised. To test the hypotheses and characteristics of the data, some standard statistical tools were used. The statistical tools such as t-test, F-ratio and correlation were used. From the analysis the result concluded that the students have positive attitude towards audio-visual aids used by the teachers.

REFERENCES

1. Glee Harrah Cady and Pat Mc Gregor (2005) “Internet is a network of network and the internet mostly connects network of computers”. Journal of research in science teaching.
2. Barry (2006) “Relationship between students perceptions of their science class room learning environment and attitude”, Journal of Educational Research.
3. Schafer (2007) vargo students science attitudes and self concept in science as a function of rose specific pupil/teacher interpersonal compatibility”, San Francisco, California, National association for research in science teaching.
4. Williams (2008), “Attitude of high school pupils towards general science

and its relationship with achievement and its subjects". Journal Community and Guidance.

5. Martis Anandi (2009), in test on scientific attitudes (TOSA), taking the point of view that attitudes must be inferred from the behavior of students, Journal of All India Association for Educational Research, Vol.17, Nos. 1 & 2, March & June.
6. Mohanty Ajay Kumar (2010), Attitudes towards education, critical thinking ability and specific effective behavious, Journal of all India Association for Educational Research, Vol.14, Nos.3 & 4.

❒

10.

Awareness on Digital Techniques Applying in Classroom Teaching for Present Generation among Teacher Educators

INTRODUCTION

Modernization is generally regarded as a process of change of traditional society into a society based on technology. As Teaching has entered the Digital age over the last several years, Technology in the Classroom is an area that all Teachers and Students are Embracing. For Teachers who have taught many years before this can be a challenging one. There are many Computer lesson plans, CDs, DVDs, audio e-books and videos available that will help in the transition. Digital Technology in the Classroom involves a lot of time and focus in its infancy, but with the Computer Lesson plans mentioned, it will develop into a fun and creative learning experience for Students and new and exciting challenges for Teachers. The incorporation of Digital technology in the education sector is important to meet the challenges presented by new trends, especially with the Global Communication of Knowledge. It is essential that the Students become familiar with the concept and use of Computer Technology in order to equip them for future job market. Similarly, the teacher can achieve better quality in Teaching Methodology.

RATIONALE OF THE STUDY

Computer plays key role in Education. Learning through Computer is an interesting affair. Now–a-days Digital Technology in Education has become the essential part of the system. In fact Teacher must well aware of the potentiality of the Digital Technology. Government is very much interested in introducing

Computer Technology in Class Room instruction in Teacher Education. Hence the Investigator was interested to know the level of Awareness on Digital techniques applying in classroom teaching for present generation among Teacher Educators.

STATEMENT OF THE PROBLEM

The important key words used in this problem were i) **Awareness:** Alertness, New Idea. ii) **Digital Technology**: The Technology which is used to change the method of Class Room Teaching with the help of Electronic machines and Computer, iii) **Teacher Educators** Teachers who are working in the Colleges of Education.

OVERVIEW OF THE STUDY ALREADY DONE

Askin Asan(2003) studied on "Computer Technology Awareness by Elementary School Teachers: A Case Study from Turkey" and found that many Teachers were not computer users. At the same time Wheatley, (2003) also studied on increasing computer use in early childhood Teacher Education. The study was found that Teachers lacked a functional Computer Literacy Foundation to new Technology and skills. Nickish and Reinhard (1992) in their study "Teacher Anxiety toward Computer Technology" found that Urban Teachers are used Computer often than Rural Teachers.

OBJECTIVES OF THE STUDY

The objectives of the study were i) To measure the level of Awareness on Digital Technology among Teacher Educators. ii) To measure the level of significant difference on the Awareness on Digital Technology among Male and Female, Rural and Urban, Science and Arts group Teacher Educators.

METHOD AND MATERIALS

It is the Normative Survey method. Investigator constructed a Tool Awareness on Digital Techniques applying in Classroom Teaching for present generation among Teacher Educators. That consists of 40 statements with different dimensions such as Computer in Teaching Learning, Power point Presentation and Internet, which have four point scale such a Strongly Agree, Agree, Disagree and Strongly Disagree. After the Development of the Questionnaire, the Investigator distributed it to Teacher Educators for validation. Their valuable ideas were taken care. Then the questionnaire was given to 10 Teacher Educators by Test - Retest method. The obtained r value 0.84 reveals that the tool is reliable one. Investigators randomly selected 100 Teacher Educators from various Colleges of Education in Perambalur and Trichy Districts.

ANALYSIS

The collected data was analysed by using different statistical technique like Mean, SD and 't' test. The results are given in the following Tables

Table 1: Significant Difference on the Mean Scores of Male and Female Teacher Educators

S.No	Dimension	Gender	Mean	SD	t test	Remarks
1.	**Total**	Male Female	64.3 63.0	0.74 0.92	**7.38**	S
2.	**CTL**	Male Female	60.54 61.62	1.19 1.41	1.48	NS
3.	**PPT**	Male Female	65.04 61.24	3.89 0.98	**6.43**	S
4.	**INT**	Male Female	71.07 69.58	1.92 3.35	**2.38**	S

CTL – Computer in Teaching Learning **PPT** – Power Point Presentation
INT Internet **NS** - Not Significant **S** - Significant

From the above Table it is noted that the 't' values are significantly difference at 5% level of the Teacher Educators for Total, PPT(Power Point Presentation) and INT(Internet). Total, PPT (Power Point Presentation) and INT (Internet) the Mean score of Male Teacher Educators are higher than the Female Teacher Educators. In CTL (Computer in Teaching Learning) there is no significant difference at 5 % level of the Teacher Educators.

Table 2: Significant Difference on the Mean Scores of Rural and Urban Teacher Educators

S.No	Dimension	Locality	Mean	SD	t test	Remarks
1.	**Total**	Rural Urban	64.7 63.07	0.837 0.823	**5.46**	S
2.	**CTL**	Rural Urban	60.74 63.18	1.61 0.989	1.69	NS
3.	**PPT**	Rural Urban	62.90 63.07	0.78 0.65	1.06	NS
4.	**INT**	Rural Urban	74.53 70.93	1.72 1.68	**3.62**	S

From the above Table, the calculated 't' values are reveal that there is no significant difference at 5% level for the dimensions CTL and PPT. But there exists significant difference at 5% level with respect to Total and INT. In the Total and INT the Mean score of the Rural Teacher Educators are higher having higher awareness on Digital Technology than the Urban Teacher Educators.

Table 3: Significant Difference on the Mean Scores of Science and Arts Teacher Educators

S.No	Dimension	Subject	Mean	SD	t test	Remarks
1.	**Total**	Science Arts	63.83 64.31	0.929 0.779	1.21	NS
2.	**CTL**	Science Arts	62.43 61.28	1.06 1.11	**4.79**	**S**
3.	**PPT**	Science Arts	63.02 60.34	4.22 0.934	**3.27**	**S**
4.	**INT**	Science Arts	71.94 73.38	1.19 1.02	**6.03**	**S**

The Mean scores and the calculated 't ' values from the above table shows that there is significant difference in all the mean score of CTL, PPT and INT at 5% level except Total. It can be understood that the level Awareness on Digital Technology among Teacher Educators are good in CTL, PPT and INT.

RESULTS AND DISCUSSION

The salient findings of the study are i) All the Teacher Educators am having good Awareness on Digitaol Technology. ii) The Mean score of Male Teacher Educators are higher than the Female Teacher Educators towards Awareness on Digital Technology with respect to the dimensions such as Total, PPT and INT. iii) With regards to Locality, the Mean score of Rural Teacher Educators are higher than the Urban Teacher Educators towards Awareness on Digital Technology in Total and INT. iv) The Mean scores of Teacher Educators with respect to Science Subject are higher in CTL, PPT and Arts Teacher Educators are higher in INT.

The result shows that Gender, Locality and Subject of Teacher Educators were not the influencing factor in determining Awareness on Digital Technology. While considering the Gender, Male Teachers are having higher Awareness on Digital Technology than the Female Teachers. This is because Male Teacher Educators may have more time to work in the Computer but the Female Teachers have the commitment to look after their family. By this way Rural Teachers are having Good Awareness on Digital Technology than the Urban Teachers. This is due to the fact that Rural Teachers may show more interest to know about the new things. As well as Science Group Teacher Educators are show more awareness than Art Group Teacher Educators. It may be due to their subject knowledge.

RECOMMENDATIONS FOR POLICY MAKINGS

The result of this study shows that the Teacher Educators are having Good awareness on Digital Technology. Hence the usage of Computer must be increased to develop their practical knowledge. They are having more involvement in using Digital Technology in their class room Teaching. Effective teaching to promote better learning, proper orientation training Programme must be provided them to develop their knowledge in Digital Technology. The Government must ensure proper training to Teacher Educators to maintain Computers and Electronic things. Educational Authorities should create, improve and sustain the Awareness of Teacher Educators about Computer Knowledge. Teacher Educators should be encouraged by Administrators to use the stand alone Computer Applications in their Teachings. Using Internet application should be given special concentration, because, it empowers and enhance creativity. Digital Technology acts as a catalyst to support change in Teacher Pedagogy.

CONCLUSION

The Good Awareness on Computer Technology among Primary and Middle School Teachers will show the Conducing Climate towards Educational Technology. The Instruction through Computer has been making wonders in the Class Room Activities. Hence Teachers must have Awareness on Computer Technology to get success and enjoy their Professions.

REFERENCE

1. Best,J.W,(2003). *Research in Education,* Prentice – Hall of India (P) Ltd., New Delhi.
2. Lokesh Koul.(2005). *Methodology of Educational Research*, Vikas Publishing House (P) Ltd, New Delhi.
3. Singh.Y.K,(2005). *Instructional Technology In Education,* A.P.H Publishing Corporation, New Delhi-110002.
4. Sareen.N, (2005). *Information and Communication Technology*, Anmol Publication Pvt.Ltd, New Delhi-110002.

❐

11.

Access to Teaching Learning Materials (TLM) among the General and Special Education Teachers in the School System

INTRODUCTION

Teaching Learning Materials (TLM) are the supportive sources for the learners to learn the contents. Some of the TLMs are customized where as others are readily available in the markets. Teachers are innovating and developing TLM according to the needs of the learners.

Learners should be the center of instruction and learning. The role of teachers is to help learners to learn. Teachers have to follow the curriculum and provide, make, or choose materials. They may adapt, supplement, and elaborate on those materials and also monitor the progress and needs of the students.

Materials include textbooks, video and audio tapes, computer software, and visual aids. They influence the content and the procedures of learning. The choice of deductive vs inductive learning, the role of memorization, the use of creativity and problem solving, production vs. reception, and the order in which materials are presented are all influenced by the materials.

Teaching materials is a generic term used to describe the resources teachers use to deliver instruction. Teaching materials can support student learning and increase student success. Ideally the teaching materials will be tailored to the content in which they are being used to the students and the teacher in the class. Teaching materials come in many shapes and sizes, but they all have in common the ability to support student learning.

Teaching materials here refers to teaching aids used when teachers carryout their activities in class room such as chalk ,writing board, charts, apparatus , specimens , concrete materials, photographs, pictures , maps ,globes , cassettes , video recording, transparencies , projectors and computers.

Materials in the typical general Education Classroom tend to be limited. Text books, work books and work sheets are the materials commonly available in the class room. Globe, Videos, soft ware and internet resources are rarely available with many of the class rooms. Braille texts, large print texts, CDs with Audio output, sign and symbols are the materials required for children having certain limitations to learn the subjects. Universally Design Learning Materials gives students the multiple means of representation of concepts and multiple means of expression for the students to demonstrate what they have learned. Instruction is flexible and provides accessibility for all students.

Every learning material we develop will be an asset for us. An investment of time or money in good teaching materials is an investment in good teaching. This study will focus on magnitude of availability and accessibility of teaching learning materials with the teachers who are interacting with the students including children with special needs.

REVIEW OF LITERATURE

Halil Eksi (2008) conducted a case study on the use of materials by classroom teachers at primary education level. They stated that they carryout various activities for an efficient and effective education and teaching, the teachers use different materials in lesson in order to create a multi learning setting for students. They face many problems while using the materials. They also reported that the newly adapted education programme requires more material use. They also reported that the insufficient materials will create problem in future.

Nelson(2006) reported that every student needs and has the right to access the curriculum regardless of disabilities or differentiated learning styles.

Pisha and Coyne (2001) identified an approach called "Smart from the start" that is Universally Designed Learning Materials (UDL) should be part of the Curriculum Learning Environments and assessments

Prema P (2009) Conducted an impact study on instructional and nurturing effect of Activity Based Learning on selected districts in Tamil Nadu and reported that the ABL method of learning influences the children's overall academic performance, improvement in reading, writing and numerical skills

Rose Meyer &Hitchcock, (2006) reported that the Alternative formats of basic materials can also be provided for students with disabilities. Such as Braille text for students with Visual Impairments , large print text for students with low vision , and CD s with audio output for students with dyslexia

Santhanam.P (2005) conducted a study on remedial programmers for children with learning difficulties in Chennai, Thiruvallur and Kancheepuram District of

Tamil Nadu and reported that the intellectual capacity of the children with learning ability is significantly higher than those with learning disability. The children with learning disability show better academic performance after remedial programme. Awareness on remedial programme about learning disabilities to be conducted through print and electronic media

Aim and Objective

The main aim is to find out the accessibility of teaching learning materials to the general and special education teachers

1. To find out the availability of teaching and learning materials in the class room for general and special education teachers
2. To find out the accessibility of teaching learning materials in the class room to teach the children.
3. To find out the incidence of using the teaching learning materials in the class room by general and special education teachers

Samples

Purposive sampling 149 teachers consisting of 82 General Education Teachers from 5 different schools and 67 Special Education Teachers working in SSA Projects up to secondary level were selected for this study.

Tool

A questionnaire consisting of 28 teaching learning materials widely used in general education and special education programme is constructed and administered with the guidelines of scoring each items on Available and used frequently (2) Available but used rarely (1) Not available (0).

Procedure

The tool was constructed and administered on the general and special education teachers working in public school by indicating their choice on each items of Teaching Learning Material in the following manner Available and used frequently (2) Available but used rarely (1) Not available (0). The confidentiality on their response is promised by the author.

Result and discussion

After collecting information from the teachers the scores were tabulated and interpreted for the study. It is learnt that the materials of Chalk and board, Chart &flash cards models, work book, poster and text are commonly available and frequently used by both general and special education teachers. Computer, laptop is available and frequently used by the general education teachers where as ABL materials, mobility aids and sign languages are frequently used by the special education teachers.

Pictures/Icons, graphics are rarely used materials by the general education teachers where as video, TV, tape, laptop, signature guide; adapted pencils are used rarely by the special education teachers. Braille, Abacus, mobility cane, sign language and ABL materials are not used by general education teachers. Whereas Computers, laptop, animation, graphics, film and slides are not used by the special education teachers. Films and graphics are not used by general and special education teachers respectively.

Table I: Access to TLM among the general and special education teachers Frequency distribution

Sl.No.	Variable	Access to TLMs by the Educators			Access to TLMs by Special educators			Total
		Not used	Rarely used	Frequently used	Not used	Rarely used	Frequently used	
1	Chalk board	0	3	79 96%		2	65 97%	149
2	Chart and flash card	6	0	76 92%	1	7	59 88%	149
3	Models	6	11	65 79%	9	19	39 58%	149
4	Video	71	5	6 7%	16	42	9 13%	149
5	Television	73	5	4 4%	16	32	19 28%	149
6	Film	77	5	0	39	22	6 8%	149
7	audio	58	10	14 17%	20	29	18 26%	149
8	Slide	67	4	11 13%	35	26	6 8%	149
9	Tape	51	15	16 19%	19	29	19 28%	149
10	Work Book	12	7	63 76%	9	18	40 59%	149
11	Poster	19	12	51 62%	29	22	16 23%	149
12	Text	10	01	71 86%	16	15	36 53%	149
13	Braille	57	04	21 25%	29	30	08 11%	149
14	Abacus	63	03	16 19%	27	24	16 23%	149
15	Mobility Can	75	02	05 6%	25	29	13 19%	149
16	Sign language	64	03	15 18%	12	23	32 47%	149
17	ABL	46	08	28 34%	09	08	50 74%	149
18	Mobility Aid	60	06	16 19%	23	18	26 38%	149
19	Book rest	47	08	27 32%	25	28	14 20%	149
20	Signature guide	19	28	35 42%	29	23	15 22%	149
21	stencils	40	22	20 24%	27	23	17 25%	149
22	Tripod pencil or pen	20	16	46 56%	23	23	20 29%	149

23	Computer	14	16	52 63%	25	23	19 28%	149
24	Adapted key board mouse	27	17	38 44%	35	19	13 19%	149
25	laptop	31	25	26 31%	28	28	11 16%	149
26	animation	36	30	16 19%	36	25	06 8%	149
27	Pictures/ Icon	20	41	21 25%	28	21	18 26%	149
28	Graphics	29	38	15 18%	60	7	0	149

Conclusion

Majority of the TLM which is used in the public schools are traditionally prepared in nature which is used regularly. The innovated materials which are available in the public school to teach the students with diversified needs are minimal and used rarely. Use of computer for teaching and learning is more common with the general education teachers than the special education teachers.

Recommendation

Teachers working in the public school system need to understand the shift from using traditional materials to the innovated materials according to the needs of children with diversified in nature. The materials need to be explored by the teachers and the students as well to optimize the learning. Use of computer should be practiced by the special education teachers for successful mainstreaming. The management may give the liberty to explore and innovate the materials according to the needs of the diversified group of learning. In-service training may be organized to innovate and develop TLM to cater the diversified group of learners. There is a need to conduct more study in this area to innovate and develop appropriate TLM which is access to all categories of learners and the teachers.

References

1. Allwright, R. L. (1990). What do we want teaching materials for? In R. Rossner and R. Bolitho, (Eds.), Currents in language teaching. Oxford University Press
2. Halil Eksi (2008) A case study on the use of materials by classroom teachers ,Kasim Yildirim
3. Educational Sciences Theory and Practice 8(1) January 2008 ,305-322
4. Pisha and Coyne (2001) Incorporating Universal Design for learning principles in to the class room design.
5. Prema P (2009) Instructional and nurturant effect of Activity Based Learning An impact study in selected districts of Tamil Nadu. SSA TN Report
6. Santhanam.P (2005). Remedial programmers for children with learning difficulties. SSA TN Report.

❐

12.

Effectiveness of E-Content in Teaching of Biological Science Education

INTRODUCTION

The development of Science and Technology, especially the application of information and communication technology (ICT) in the new era has greatly influenced teaching and learning in education. In the present era of knowledge explosion, adopting modern tools for teaching is one of the predominant needs of the hour. Instructional technology in the third world is changing rapidly. Knowledge packaging in electronic form or e-content is a powerful technique for teaching all subjects. ICT have become handy in class room teaching which has the potential to engage the students throughout the period and make learning easy and effective through, visual aids, animations and simulations.

NEED FOR THE STUDY

New innovations are coming to the fields of education in terms of technology which promises to change the process of teaching and learning. Training of competent teachers is very important because they directly or indirectly influence the quality and the quantity of educational services. Without adequately trained teacher cadre the institution cannot aim to expand the educational facilities.

E-CONTENT

The term 'e-content' refers to that form of knowledge or content which is packed in an electronic form. It includes text, audio, video, animations, images etc. An innovative application of computer in the teaching and learning process is e-content. E-content is the advancement of technology to design, deliver, select, administer and extend learning.

OBJECTIVES OF THE STUDY

1. To prepare e-content for particular topic in Teaching of Biological Science Education at B.Ed., level.
2. To find out whether there is any significant difference in achievement means score between control group and experimental group in learning Teaching of Biological Science Education by the B.Ed., student teachers.

METHODOLOGY

The investigator followed the experimental method for the present study. The data thus collected were put into appropriate statistical analysis: Mean, t-test, standard deviation.

SAMPLING PROCEDURE

The present study is concerned only with B.Ed student teachers in J.J. College of Education and Oxford College of Education, Trichy. Hence the college selected could be considered as a representative college. Eighteen students have been selected for experimental group and another eighteen students for control group by using purposive sampling method.

HYPOTHESES OF THE STUDY

The following hypotheses were formulated based on the objectives of the study

1. There is no significant difference in the Posttest achievement mean scores between control group and experimental group.
2. There is significant difference in the achievement mean scores between the Pre and Post test of experimental groups who learnt through e-content.

Table 1: The table shows the comparison of Post-test achievement mean scores of Experimental group and control group.

Group Compared	N	M	SD	t value	df	Level of significance
Control Group	18	8.72	1.127	9.22	34	**Significant**
Experimental Group	18	13.33	1.910			

The calculated t-value 9.22 is greater than the critical value 2.704 corresponding to the 0.01 level of significance. This implies that the control group and experimental group differ significantly in their achievement in the post-test. Hence the null hypothesis is not accepted.

Table 2: The table shows the difference between the Pre-test and Post-test achievement mean scores due to treatment for the experimental group.

Experimental Group	No of students	Mean	SD	't' value	df	Level of significance
Pre – test	18	10.72	1.364	8.040	34	**Significant**
Post - test	18	13.33	1.910			

The calculated t-value 8.040 is greater than the critical value 2.704 corresponding to the 0.01 level of significance. This shows that experimental group is highly significant in their achievement in post-test. Hence the null hypothesis is accepted.

MAJOR FINDINGS OF THE STUDY

The major findings which have emerged from the study are as follows:

1. An Achievement test was conducted to access the effectiveness of the e-content. While analyzing the result, i.e., the performance of the students in the achievement test is better and it became clear that the e-content is effective.
2. The student teachers of experimental group who were taught through e-content achieved more in subject units than the control group student teachers.
3. It was found .that learning through e-content and learning through traditional lecture method are not similar and they differ significantly.

EDUCATIONAL IMPLICATIONS OF THE STUDY

1. New instructional techniques of assisting student through computer are to be explored by the teachers and researchers continuously.
2. Teachers of higher secondary schools can be given orientation as how to develop e-content.
3. The use of e-content is found to be valid in enhancing the achievement; it will diminish wastage and stagnation in school.

CONCLUSION

Based on the proceeding findings of the study, the following conclusions are arrived.

The levels of performance of teacher trainees who learnt through e-content were greater the other part and hence it was evident that e-content is also an effective approach to teach Biological Science Education. The rise of e-learning and an electronic content (e-content) is a new paradigm for education and training in the knowledge society, empowered by technological advancements which give the modern instructional technology. The development of educational content in time with the changing times has become a major responsibility of the modern teacher who has to face a new learner in a new environment. More over the level of motivation, learning style and anxiety towards computer improves the efficiency of the student teachers and hence the e-content approach is having great scope in the instructional design of the student teachers.

REFERENCES

1. Jeya Shanmuga Raja. J, E-Content Development on Teaching method of Zoology at B.Ed Level., Paper presented at the *International conference on Quality Enhancement in Distance Education for LifeLong Learning* 26-27 Mar.2011.
2. Suma.S.(2007). Development and Validation of e-content on the uses of the simple present tense in English at higher secondary level. M.Phil Thesis submitted to Bharathidasan University.
3. Udayakumar.P, Impact of Multimedia Technology in Learning Biological Science on B.Ed. Trainees, http://www.languageinindia.com/feb2013/udayakumarfinal.pdf saved on 14.5.13

❐

13.

Learning Styles of Higher Secondary Students in Biological Science in Villupuram District

INTRODUCTION

Learning style is a hypothetical contract that has been developed to explain the process of mediation between stimuli and response. Learning style as on integral concept that bridges the personality cognitive dimensions of the individuals. The learning styles are synonymous. He defines learning styles as the course of learning. Laycock (1978) describes learning styles as an individual characteristic way of responding to certain variable in the instructional environment. In simplest terms, a students learning style is the peculiar way with which he learns best. The present study aims to find out the learning styles of higher secondary students in biological science in Villupuram District. A samples of 100 respondents selected randomly were studied. A questionnaire method of survey was used to find out the learning styles of higher secondary students in biological science. The data were collected by using questionnaire as an instrument. Primary data were collected by conducting direct structured interview using questionnaire. All the respondents were asked the same questions in the same fashion and they were informed the purpose of study. Regression and correlation analysis were applied to test the hypotheses. The data collected through questionnaires have been tabulated. The findings and observations are the result and outcome of the interpretations made during the study of analysis. The result found that average learning styles of higher secondary students in biological science in Villupuram District.

The act or experience of one that learns. Knowledge or skill acquired by instruction or study. Modification of a behavioral tendency by experience (as exposure to conditioning).

Adapted from How Learning Works by Ambrose et al.: an engagingly written, evidence-based text, well-illustrated by practical examples, and a book well worth your time, as a TA and as a student.

As teachers, our goal is to encourage learning in our classrooms. But what is learning, and what principles or factors affect how our students learn? In this section, we provide you with the very basics of what learning is, how and when it occurs, and how to structure your lessons to maximize student learning.

There are three components to the definition of Learning:

1. **"Learning is a process, not a product."** Exam scores and term papers are measures of learning, but they are not the process of learning itself.
2. **"Learning is a change in knowledge, beliefs, behaviors or attitudes."** This change requires time, particularly when one is dealing with changes to core beliefs, behaviors, and attitudes. Don't interpret a lack of sea change in your students' beliefs or attitudes immediately following a lesson as a lack of learning on their part, but instead, consider that such a change will take time – perhaps a few weeks, perhaps until the end of the term, or even longer.
3. **"Learning is not something done to students, but something that students themselves do."** If you have ever carefully planned a lesson, only to find that your students just didn't "get it," consider that your lesson should be designed not just to impart knowledge but also to lead students through the process of their own learning.

Learning is the process by which one acquires, ingests, and stores or accepts information. Our experiences with learned information compose our bodies of knowledge. Learning is a process unique to each individual. Some learn quickly, scanning the information and mastering the concept or skill seemingly effortlessly. Others stumble while processing information, taking longer to grasp the concept or requiring numerous exposures over a sustained period of time. Some individuals store the information they've learned indefinitely, cementing it in their memories. Others find that the information they've learned slips away rapidly. Some learn best through text, others through practice, some through hearing. Learning styles are as unique and varied as our personalities. Learning is a lifelong endeavor. As long as one remains engaged in life, learning does not cease.

Until recently most people took learning styles for granted and left them to instinct. Realization that studying how learning should come before everything else is spreading in the world of education skill in this field can multiply efficiency. The use of higher level work skills can bring improvement in almost all fields. Improvement in athletic field and industrial productivity have been achieved in the way. Everyone is familiar with the difference in output of a self-taught typist who uses one finger of each hand and an expert who was taught the tough system. Other experiments has shown that the level of performance on such tasks as card sorting, pitch discrimination and puzzle solving is affected by the method employed and the limit to performance might be improved of better work was used.

These findings on effects of work methods on levels of performance led to the significant theoretical contribution to theories regarding the causes of individual difference in competence. It was long assumed that these differences were primarily due to two factors. (1) Learning and (2) Amount of training in a task. Dr. Seashare after studying may findings on effects of work method, concluded that method of work was a third variable in instruction. It is found that new levels in achievement are possible by improving the learning styles.

Both in common speech and educational literature the word "Read" is used to designate a wide variety of learned activities from the socially undesirable to the highly ethnical, form bodily skill, such as walking to mental activities such as learning of critical thinking and from specified abilities to generalized attitudes. The meaning of learning includes the ideal of facility in the performance of an act, combined with a persisting inclination towards the repetition of the act.

As Bagley has said "To teach a child to study effectively is to do that most valuable thing that could be done to help him adjust himself to any environment of modern civilized life into which they live. In 1917 strays and Newsworthy declared "Many teachers have taught subjects, but not how to study subjects, the latter is more important". H.R. Bhatia says, "unless opportunities for doing and respecting things are afforded to children it is futile to expect them to form habits". Sevmors and exhortations may help children to acquire normal vocabulary but not normal character. Percepta in the formation of learning unless children are afforded actual practice in those modes behaviour.

REVIEW OF LITERATURE

Mary Lou Koran, John J. Koran (2006), conducted a study "Interaction of Learner aptitudes with question packing in learning from prose, he suggested that, in some cases, reduction in certain information Processing requirements may actually be an important prerequisite to affective utilization of other aptitudes (learning).

The over-all means used in the analysis are presented, both low and high aptitude students in "favourable" classrooms had higher achievements scores than the two groups in 'unfavourable' classroom. This contexts effect was present to some extent in both third and fourth grade class room aptitude, third grade students. It appears that being in a classroom with many high-aptitude students is beneficial for low-aptitude students and some high-aptitude students as well".

K.S Kahlon and Vinod Uppalo, (2007) studied on "women's aptitude and achievement in Relation to achievement motivation.

The Result of the present investigation fully support the hypotheses on the basis of which the study had been undertaken.

1. There is significant, but imperfect relationship between aptitude (learning style) and academic achievement.
2. Discrepancy between aptitude (Learning style) and achievement bears no relationship with ability.
3. Discrepancy between aptitude (Learning Style) and achievement bears significant relationship with academic achievement.
4. Discrepancy between aptitude and achievement bears significant relationship with achievement motivation. That is, high achievement motivation goes with positive discrepancy where as low achievement motivation accounts for negative discrepancy"

Robert B. Burnes (2012) conducted a study on "The Relation of Aptitudes of Learning at different Points in the time during Instruction: The result of this study suggested that some aptitude-learning relations are not stable over time and that his instability is exhibited in different aptitudes being required at different points in time during instruction. These findings supported most of the Junior evidence examining aptitude correlates at different stages of learning and did not support the assumption made in ATI Research that aptitudes relate equally to learning for the during of treatment"

Moraddwaj Varma (2013) conducted a study on "Comparative achievement in science of Tharu Tribals and other at high school level. He found, that the achievement of Tharu tribals is lower than that of the non-tharus in all the three science subjects were significant at .01 level"

In **Jamur (2013)** made a study in Patna in relationship between study habits and achievement. His study showed a correlation of 0.51 between study habits and achievement of students and a correlation of 0.144 between study habits and intelligence.

OBJECTIVES

1. To study the higher secondary learning styles in Biological science.
2. To know the higher secondary different methods learning styles in Biological science.
3. To find out the higher secondary factors learning styles in Biological science.

METHODOLOGY

The methodology adopted for the study is explained in detail. The sampling technique, size of the sample, variables of the study, description of the tool used and administration of tool are elaborated.

Sample

The sample selected for the present study is 100 higher secondary students in Villupuram district. Random sampling technique was used for the selection of sample.

Data Collection

Primary data, required for the present research work were collected by conducting direct interviews using questionnaire. All the respondents were given sufficient information about the Project work. These respondents were provided with the same questionnaires. They were also informed that they have to answer in the same fashion.

Tools used in the Study

SOLAT Tool of learning style D. Venketraman (1986) consists of 25 items. The learning style comprises 5 categories.

1. Verbal (1 to 5 items)
2. Content preference (6 to 10 items)
3. Class preference (11 to 15 items)
4. Learning preference (16 to 20 items)
5. Interest (20 to 25 items)

Scoring Procedure

1. The maximum score that a student obtains is 50 the minimum score that a student gain is 25.
2. Each item has two alternatives. If the student chooses the First alternative one mark is given. If the student chooses Second alternative the student it secures 2 marks. The first alternative of an item indicates the use of Right hemisphere of the brain and the second alternative of an item indicates the use of left hemisphere of the brain.

Tool validity and reliability

The main attributes needed to be considered regarding a good tool are validity and reliability.

Validity: A measuring instrument is said to be valid if it measures what it purpose to measure. Validity may be defined as the extent to which an instrument or a test does the job derived of it.

The kind of validity and the extent or degrees to which it should be established are the major consideration while establishing validity.

In the present study the researcher found out the content validity.

Content validity gives the logical evidence that the content of the items of a test is suitable for the purpose for which the test is designed and used. Content validity is established is 0.549.

Reliability

The efficiency of measuring the different items are called on aspect of reliability. Reliability determined test-retest method and it is found to be validity of the tool is (0.82).

HYPOTHESIS

1. The level of learning styles among higher secondary students on the basis of their demographic variables.
2. The level of different method learning styles among higher secondary students on the basis of their demographic variables.
3. The level of factors learning styles among higher secondary students on the basis of their demographic variables.

ANALYSIS AND INTERPRETATION

Table 1: Showing the Stepwise regression analysis predicting learning styles among higher secondary students and demographic variables

Sl.No	Step/Source	Unstandardized Coefficients Beta	Std. Error	Standardized Coefficients Beta Beta	Step t	P
1.	Gender	1.342	0.343	1.245	5.432	0.01
2.	Locality	1.224	0.392	0.269	6.641	0.01
3.	Family Income	1.924	0.549	0.149	4.142	0.01
4.	Father Education	2.334	0.667	0.108	5.339	0.01

* $P < 0.01$

Four variables viz Gender, Locality, Family income and Father Education have significantly contributed for predicting the learning styles among higher secondary students. The Gender seems to be 5.432, Locality seems to be 6.641, Family income seems to be 4.142 and Father education seems to be 5.339. The predictive value of these variables separately is 0.01.

Table 2: Showing the Stepwise regression analysis predicting different method learning styles and demographic variables

Sl.No	Step/Source	Unstandardized Coefficients Beta	Std. Error	Standardized Coefficients Beta Beta	Step t	P
1.	Type of Family	1.133	0.505	0.434	2.246	0.01
2.	Religion	1.248	0.466	0.782	2.677	0.01
3.	Community	1.792	0.683	0.646	2.625	0.01
4.	Birth Place	2.338	0.670	0.954	3.490	0.01

* $P < 0.01$

Four variables viz Type of family, Religion, Community and Birth place have significantly contributed for predicting the method learning styles. The first variable Type of family seems to be 2.246, Religion seems to be 2.677, Community seems to be 2.625 and Birth place seems to be 3.490. The predictive value of these variables separately is 0.01.

Table 3: Showing the Stepwise regression analysis predicting factors learning styles among higher secondary students and demographic variables

Sl.No	Step/Source	Unstandardized Coefficients Beta	Std. Error	Standardized Coefficients Beta Beta	Step t	P
1.	Gender	5.195	1.030	0.824	5.041	0.01
2.	Family Monthly Income	1.809	0.451	0.443	4.016	0.01

* P < 0.01

Two variables viz Gender and Family Monthly Income have significantly contributed for predicting the factors learning styles among higher secondary. The first variable Gender seems to be 5.195, when paired with the second variable Family monthly income is 1.809. The predictive value of these variables separately is 0.01.

Table 4: Showing the correlation between the learning styles of higher secondary students and demographic variables

Factors	Learning styles of higher secondary students
Gender	0.579*
Locality	0.782**
Family Income	0.591*
Father Education	0.572*
Type of Family	0.824**

* Significant at 0.01 level ** Significant at 0.05 level

Learning styles of higher secondary students is positively and significantly related to Gender (0.579), Locality (0.782), Family Income (0.591), Father Education (0.572) and Type of family (0.824). So the direct relationship between the Learning styles of higher secondary students and demographic variables.

CONCLUSION

The present study aims to find out the higher secondary students learning styles. The researcher framed objectives and hypotheses on the basis of the above context. The research was carried out in 100 samples based randomly. A questionnaire constructed by R was used to collect the relevant data. After collecting the data they were analyzed using statistical tools such as Regression and Correlation analysis. The result concluded that students have average level of learning styles at Higher Secondary level in Biological science in Villupuram District.

REFERENCES

1. Hammet Gandhi, H. & Varma, M. (2008). Elucidating Mathematical problem solving through met cognition. Journal of Indian Education, 30(3).
2. Kaholan & Vinod uppal, (2007) Womens attitude and achievement in relation to achievement motivation, Journal of Education and Psychology, Vol. xxxviii, No 3: 198-201.
3. Live, Carl (2008) Formative Assessment Pre- Test to Identify College students' Prior Knowledge, Misconceptions and Learning Difficulties in Biology. International Journals of Science and Mathematics Vol.4.
4. LongDon, Bernard (2013) Genetics - Are there inherent learning difficulties?
5. Lovelace, M. K. (2005). Meta-Analysis of Experimental Research Based on the Dunn and Dunn Model. Journal of Educational Research, 98(3), 176-183.
6. Malini, Sujatha (2006) The Attitude of special and Normal School Teachers towards children with Disabilities.
7. Mary Lou Koran, John J. Koran (2006) Individual and teacher/class effects in aptitude treatment studies, American Educational Research Journal, Vol.17, No.3: 291-302.
8. Mary Lou Koran, John J. Koran (2006) Individual and teacher/class effects in aptitude treatment studies, American Educational Research Journal, Vol.17, No.3: 291-302.
9. Robert B. Burns, (2012) The relation of aptitude to learning at different points in the time during instruction, Journal of Educational Psychology, Vol. 72, No.6: 705-789.

❐

14.

Awareness of Flip Teaching among School Teachers in and Around Madurai District

INTRODUCTION

"A Quality education has the power to transform societies in a single generation, provide children with the protection they need from the hazards of poverty, labor exploitation and disease and give them the knowledge, skills and confidence to reach their full potential". India needs multi-dimensional and broad based quality education to maintain its leader ship in the 21st century. Therefore India should show the concern over the quality in education as the education in India is not competitive in terms of the quality with other countries. The FLIP classroom is the latest learning model to have taken the teaching and training world by storm.

In a flipped classroom content normally delivered in lectures is covered by students in their own time, often through the use of video or readings. Face-to-face time is used for activities where the focus is on learning through experience. It allows teachers and trainers to flip through concepts, which in turn gives them more time to interact with students instead of lecturing. This is also known as backwards classroom, reverse instruction, flipping the classroom and reverse teaching. The flip classroom is ideal for adult education and training, where students are more self-motivated and focused. This model of learning compliments training objectives which are 'actionable' rather than passive objectives like 'awareness or comprehension'.

Significance of the Study

This study is undertaken to find out the awareness of flip teaching among school teachers in and around Madurai District. This study gave them the clear knowledge about Flip teaching is a form of blended learning in which students learn new content online by watching video lectures, usually at home, and what used to be homework (assigned problems) is now done in class with teachers offering more personalized guidance and interaction with students, instead of lecturing. This is also known as backwards classroom, flipped classroom, reverse teaching, and the Thayer Method

Background of the Study

This study was done in and around Madurai city. The need of today is quality of education. If the quality is maintained in all the above we can produce professionally skillful students who are going to the meet the future global citizens. So it is necessary to have innovative teaching methods or alternative methods in imparting knowledge among the students. The traditional pattern of teaching has been to assign students to read textbooks and work on problem sets outside school, while listening to lectures and taking tests in class.

Traditionally, the teacher engages with the students who ask questions - but those who don't ask tend to need the most attention. "We refer to 'silent failers,'" said one teacher, claiming that flipping allows her to target those who need the most help rather than the most confident. Flipping changes teachers from "sage on the stage" to "guide on the side", allowing them to work with individuals or groups of students throughout the session. The Investigator wanted to know whether there is awareness of flip teaching among school teachers in and around Madurai District

Objectives of the study

1. To measure and find out whether there is awareness of flip teaching among school teachers in and around Madurai District
2. To enable the teachers to sensitize the today's needed to turn towards the flip teaching and classrooms.

Hypotheses

1. Awareness of flip teaching among school teachers in and around Madurai District are high
2. There is significant difference in the awareness of flip teaching among school teachers with regard to the board of institution. [Matriculation and CBSE]
3. There is significant difference in the awareness of flip teaching among school teachers with regard to the gender. [Male & Female]

Methodology used

The survey method was taken and target population is the school teachers who are teaching in various boards such as Matriculation and CBSE in and around Madurai district. The size of the samples of the present study is 60 teachers.

Tool Construction

The self made check list was used to find out whether there is awareness of flip teaching among school teachers in and around Madurai District. The checklist had 20 items

Administration of the Tool

The photocopies of the check-list were distributed to the teachers of four educational institutions in and around Madurai. The filled in questionnaires were corrected analyzed and interpreted.

Statistical Technique Used

CALCULATING MEAN VALUE, 'T' TEST

Table shows the number of teachers from four schools

S.No.	Name of the school	Institution	Total no	F	M
1)	S.S.V.Sala	Matriculation	15	15	-
2)	Le Chatlier	Matriculation	15		15
3)	PVK Academy	CBSE	15	8	7
4)	Vellammal	CBSE	15	7	8
		Total	60	30	30

Hypothesis: 1

Awareness of flip teaching among school teachers in and around Madurai District is high

Table Showing the Mean Value

Name of the school	Total no	Sex		Board	Over All Mean
		Female	Male		
S.S.V.Sala	15	15	-	Matriculation	7.5
Le Chatlier	15		15	Matriculation	9
PVK Academy	15	8	7	CBSE	8.5
Vellammal	15	7	8	CBSE	9.5

It is inferred from the above table that there is no Awareness of flip teaching among school teachers in and around Madurai District .All the mean scores indicated that they are less than the theoretical mean (10). Still there were no innovative teaching methods were followed to reach the global standard as well as to improve the low achievers.

Hypothesis: 2

There is significant difference in the awareness of flip teaching among school teachers with regard to the board of institution. [Matriculation and CBSE]

Table showing the difference between the variables

S.No	Variable	Mean	Std.dev	't'	Significance at 0.5 level
1	Matriculation	8.25	0.50	0.93	No Significant
2	CBSE	9	0.74		

It is inferred from the above table that the't' value is 0.93 is lesser than the't' value 1.96 at 0.5 level of significance. So the research hypothesis is rejected. The result indicated that there is no significant difference in the awareness of flip teaching among school teachers with regard to the board of institution. [Matriculation and CBSE]

Hypothesis: 3

There is significant difference in the awareness of flip teaching among school teachers with regard to the gender. [Male & Female]

Table showing the difference between the variables

S.NO	Variable	mean	Std. dev	't'	Significance at 0.5 level
1	Female	8.5	1.25	0.98	No Significant
2	male	9	0.57		

It is inferred from the above table that the't' value is 0.98 is lesser than the't' value 1.96 at 0.5 level of significance. So the research hypothesis is rejected. The result indicated that there is no significant difference in the awareness of flip teaching among school teachers with regard to the gender. [Male & Female]

Hypotheses Verification

1. There is significant difference in the awareness of flip teaching among school teachers with regard to the board of institution. [Matriculation and CBSE] is rejected.
2. There is significant difference in the awareness of flip teaching among

school teachers with regard to the gender. [Male & Female] is rejected.

Delimitation

The samples are taken from only from four schools in and around Madurai area and also restricted to the variable that is type of institution and gender alone. In this study the Investigator use only mean and't' test as the statistical treatment .This was also delimitation.

Scope of the Study

This study can highlight the need for the alternative, creative, student friendly, user friendly and innovative methods of teaching. The flip classroom is the latest learning model to have taken the teaching and training world by storm. The flip teaching models are being incorporated by teachers of all subjects, for students of all ages. This mode of learning is now slowly making inroads into the teaching and training in India. The flip classroom is ideal for adult education and training, where students are more self-motivated and focused. This model of learning compliments training objectives which are 'actionable' rather than passive objectives like 'awareness or comprehension'.

Suggestion for the Future

1. We can take more schools for the study
2. We can take so many variables
3. We can also use extend all the boards of schools in future.

Educational Implications

This Study revealed that there is a need for considering another scenario where in students has already gone through a video lecture on the second conditional at their own time. They can rewind, pause and repeat the lecture as many times as they want. Additionally, they do graded exercises to practice the concept and take up an assessment to check their proficiency. Both the learner and the facilitator now know what to focus on and the class is much more productive for the learner. The facilitator only has to provide solutions for problem areas. Flip training can help overcome the constraints and make learning a focused and productive experience for the learner

❐

15.

Computer Assisted Instruction on Circulatory System

INTRODUCTION

Education should be an individual activity to a much greater content. Not at all children should be forced to go through the same steps of learning at the same speed. The high achievers will move faster in their learning where as the under achievers will need more time. Children have their own ways of learning. Some children may learn better through the use of different learning materials them by merely listening to an inspirational talk by the teacher. The style of learning may also change according to age. They use their season in acquiring knowledge. An important feature of education is its use of physical and intellectual tools. Education must reflect the influence of technology. This new technology demands new interpretations of the instructional process and those changed with educating the next generation must engage in a continual cycle of education and revaluation in the light of technological influence at all levels.

TECHNOLOGY IN EDUCATION

This is based on the application of engineering principle for developing electro mechanical equipment like motion pictures, tape – recorders, teaching machines, computers, television etc. This approach of education a technology is a bye product of the 21th century. **DAVIS** (1971) thinks that the hardware approach is based on the application of physical science to the education and training system which mechanics the process of teaching gradually so that teachers would be able to deal with more students resulting in less cost and economy in finances. It is said that good teachers have always used visual ads to assist their teaching ancient great masters used illustrations and models to increase the interests of their students. Today educational technology is stressing modern audio – visual and computer equipment.

TECHNOLOGY OF EDUCATION

It refers to the study of principles and theories, formulate to solve problems in the teaching, learning process. The main frame work of education technology is provided by Technology or Education. 'Technology in Education' provides the support to implement the broader instructional design. It primarily implies systematic approach to instructional design incorporating alternative methodologies, media and aids with reference to the objective vis-à-vis learning content. This accommodates the systems approach, programmed learning etc.

According to the **encyclopedia of education** (1971. vol-9 P.22) Educational Technology is the purposeful combination or separately of objects, techniques, devices, events and relationships to increase the effectiveness of the educational process.

APPLICATION OF EDUCATION TECHNOLOGY

Educational Technology has gradually influenced and developed the teaching learning process. Since the world is moving towards Technological growth information and special place in education. The trend is to introduce technological principles in the classroom. Educational technology consists of all modern media, methods and materials, which can be used to maximizing the learning experience of student at various levels.

HISTORICAL PERSPECTIVE OF INDIVIDUAL INSTRUCTION

The classical conditioning of **PAVLOV** opened a new chapter in teaching and learning and the behaviour gave importance to reinforcement as a major condition for learning. Edward Thorn dike improved the reinforcement procedure with stimulus (reinforce) response reaction, **SKINNER** (1967) expanded this idea as operative conditioning which led to the invention of teaching machine. Both kin aesthetic and information feedback are identified to play crucial role in skill learning by **GAGNE** (1963) **LUMSDANOE** (1964) proposed a new definition to instructional technique which was later applied in programmed instruction. The five golden rules applied in this preparation of programmed learning material (PLM) and the need for defining the objectives in behavioural terms in the preparation of instructional software material are proposed as essential by **DANIEL DAVIS** (1965). The three phases that help the teacher to decide in the ongoing focus on pedagogy are; what to teach (objectives) whom to teach (entering behaviour) and how to flash the procedures which are similar to the CAI model. **FLANDERS'** (1964) recommendation for interactivity in learning are subjoined through various learning activities built in the CAI package.

INDIVIDUALISED INSTRUCTION

Individualized instruction is the one-to-one relationship between a student and what he learns (**DUNN** and **DUNN** 1977). Individualised instruction is one of the most active areas in the education innovations. This kind of instruction helps the learner to learn at his own pace. Modern class rooms are characterized by a high degree of heterogeneity. Individual differences are pronounced among learners in large classes and to cater to the needs of the learners in such classes individualized instruction bodies is required.

Through individualized instruction materials self learning can be enhanced. This land of self learning helps the learners to learn even more difficult contents and learning of higher categories. Through self learning the needs and levels of the learners are considerably satisfied. The individual differences are considered and hence individualized instruction certainly leads to mastery level of learning. Individualized instruction may be provided for the following reasons (**DUNN** and **DUNN** 1977)

(a) A gifted student, able to come with new consents or skills independently may work well ahead of his peers through the use of this method. He need not wait to learn until the teacher can work with him individually or the rest of his peers catch up with him.

(b) An interested student may learn more about a given topic, consent or skill after most of his peers have mastered it, may spend as much time as needed reinforcing the knowledge at his desire and pace until he too is ready to move ahead.

(c) An interested student may learn more about a given topic, consents or skill at the moment in time when he wants to, not when the teacher is able to get to the subject.

(d) An average student who cares to something new in an interesting way may become sufficiently motivated to work on his own because of the nature of the varied multi sensory experience.

Individualized instruction materials should have certain characteristics. According to **MORE** (1968), an individualized instructional material should have the following features. It should as

1. Permit the learners to explore freely.
2. Inform the learner about the consequence of his action.
3. Be self – pacing that is the student can more at his own rate of learning.
4. Permit the learner to make full use of his capacity for discovering relations of various kinds.

GOLDSCHMID (1973) maintain that any form of individualized instruction should possess the following characters. It should

1. Emphasize learning
2. Ensure active students participation
3. Stress evaluation and feed back
4. Principle of individual pacing

There are different forms of individualized instruction. Some of them are

1. Learning Module
2. Multimedia Package
3. Programmed Learning Material (PLM)
4. Personalised system of instruction (PSI)
5. Audio Tutorial Instruction (ATI)

Learning Module

A learning module is a short unit of instruction dealing with a single unit of subject matter self contained with define objectives. Based on the specified instructional objectives, questions are given and the learner assesses his/her performance in the subject.

Multimedia Package

A multimedia package consists of a collection of soft ware's of several media dealing with a specific topic on subject area and forming an integrated whole. Based on the interest and aptitude of the students, the students can select the media through which they want to learn the subject.

Programmed Learning Material (PLM)

Skinner has pronounced Programmed Learning Material (PLM) based on the theory of operant conditioning PLM consists of planned sequence of learning activity for achieving mastery in terms of stimulus response reinforcement relationship.

Personalised System of Instruction (PSI)

The Personalised System of Instruction refers to training which is based on self pacing and master learning. In PSI, learners work in their own and they must achieve mastery of a series of written learning unit. They are assisted by teachers and professors. It is possible to apply PSI.

Audio Tutorial Instruction (ATI)

Here the instructor's remarks, directions and interpretations of learning assignments and resources are given through audio cassettes. The cassettes are prepared by the concerned subject experts keeping in mind the target for which the cassette is prepared. Even for distance education system, audio cassettes are being used for instruction.

A computer is programmed with linear or branching programmes. It acts like a super teaching machine catering to the needs of a number of students at the same time. The characteristic aspects of the CAI is its capacity to initiate flexible instructional with the student. In this respect it is superior to the teaching machine. The computer can do this in different ways. The computer is able to record and store all the responses of all the students. It can use the information in deciding what information is to be given to the student next. It can branch not just in terms of on answer but also in terms of a whole series of previous answers. It can also record the time taken to answer a question and the decree of correctness of the student's response. It uses the information in planning to determine which branch or format would be conductive to a learner for effective instruction.

Computer Assisted Instruction is not merely a sophisticated type of programmed instruction but a different kind of instruction but a different kind of instruction altogether. No doubt, data processing, data communication, consents of audio-visual and media theory, communication theory, system theory and learning theory are annelid in the preparation of the CAI material. In contrast to CAI, Computer Managed Instruction (CMI) analysis the relationship between various factors concerned with the learning of a pupil and suggests activities appropriate to individual students.

DIFFERENT FORMS OF COMPUTER ASSISTED INSTRUCTION

Computer Assisted Instruction can be take any one of the following modes depending on the purpose of the material, the five different modes of CAI are

(a) Drill and Practice
(b) Tutorial Mode
(c) Simulation Mode
(d) Discovery Mode
(e) Gaming Mode

Tutorial Mode

In this mode information is presented in small units followed by a question. The student's response is analysed by the computer and an appropriate feedback is provided. This is similar to programmed instruction. As in programmed instruction, the information may be given in a linear fashion as in branched pathways. The greater the number of alternative paths, more adaptive the tutorial can be to individuals.

Drill and Practice Mode

The learner, provided with a number of graded examples on the concepts and principles learnt earlier. The idea is to develop proficiency and fluency through doing all the correct responses are reinforced and the incorrect responses are diagnosed and corrected. The compute continues the drill and the learners continue his practice until mastery is achieved by the learner.

Simulation Mode

In this mode, the learners are presented with scheduled down stimulated. Situations bearing correspondence with real situation. Simulations are made to avoid risk, save money and conserve time, simulation of an aeroplane in flight, an experiment on titration, a nuclear reaction, collision of two bodies are good examples of the simulation models in science.

Discovery Mode

The individual approach to teaching and learning is as followed. The learner is encouraged to proceed through trial and error approach i.e., by solving a given problem, realizing where and how he/she went wrong, trying again and finally solving the complex problem.

Gaming Mode

In this mode, the learner is engaged in playing opposite. The computer or opposite another learner. The extent of learning depends upon the type of the game. Games on spelling names of places and general knowledge are some examples of the gaming mode.

Information Handling

One area where processing and information handling capacity of computer is profitably used in counseling and guiding the computer stores complete cumulative records and match them against employment needs and potentialities as required for personal and vocational guidance.

MERITS OF COMPUTER ASSISTED INSTRUCTION

Computer Assisted Instruction has several advantages over other systems of instructions.

1. Each student receives instruction at his own pace
2. Each student receives immediate feedback for his response
3. Each student responds continuously as he receives instruction
4. All units of learning are broke down into subunits and elements of learning in accordance with skinner's approach of teaching in small steps
5. Reinforcement of learning is achieved by personal message
6. Learning sessions are not manageable by designing the duration between half an hour to one hour
7. Student can access the computer any place
8. Students can learn in their own styles and ways
9. Students can test their own learning at any point of time to an end
10. Lesson from the theories of learning are taken into account at stage instructional design
11. Teacher's time is saved from the routine job of giving activity and employed in innovative instruction design and student guidance

OBJECTIVES OF THE STUDY

1. To understand about computer system and its working
2. To understand the educational application of computer
3. To develop scientific attitude among school students

4. To provide a broad – based biological knowledge, stimulate a deep interest in the natural world
5. To develop a CAI package for self instruction on the unit circulatory system in science for IX standard students
6. To enable the pupils to utilize effectively the instructional material in learning biology
7. To verify whether there is any difference in learning level between
   a) Boys and Girls
   b) Rural and Urban School
   c) Government, Government Aided and Unaided Schools

HYPOTHESIS

1. There is no significant difference between the pretest and posttest scores of government school pupils' following the Computer Assisted Instruction.
2. There is no significant difference between the pretest and posttest scores of Aided School Pupils' following the Computer Assisted Instruction.
3. There is no significant difference between the pretest and posttest scores of Unaided School Pupil following the Computer Assisted Instruction.
4. There is no significant difference between the pretest and posttest mean scores of the experimental group following Computer Assisted Instruction.
5. There is no significant difference in post test performance of Computer Assisted Instruction between the different types of school pupil.
6. There is no significant difference between the post test performance of Urban and Rural school pupil following Computer Assisted Instruction.
7. There is no significant difference between the post test performance of Boys and Girls following Computer Assisted Instruction.

SCOPE OF THE STUDY

1. The students can get more and adequate knowledge through self instruction material.
2. It helps the students to develop self study habits, since individual study can be brought out with the help of self instruction material.
3. The study is expected to help the students at all levels, since computer plays a vital role in all the aspects of life especially in the field of education.
4. The present study is experimental study to compose the effectiveness of CAI and on "Circulatory System" for IX standard students.
5. In future instruction materials will act as a source of the knowledge for the teacher and students.
6. It will help the teacher in the teaching learning process, as it can draw the attention of the students by teaching learning computer.

STUDIES CONDUCTED ON CAI IN INDIA

In India at present several efforts are being taken up to develop the software for CAI, for individual instruction several studies also have been conducted to identify the effectiveness of CAI and Handout over the achievement of the students. SHARMA and GEORGE (1979) developed a CAI package of mathematics. Their objectives were to study the effectiveness of the CAI for school children and the findings revealed that the CAI packages produced significant result over the achievement of the children.

BADRINATH (1986) conducted a study on developing and validating CAI package for reflection of light at the VIII standard level. He found that experience in CAI program appeared to be an effective method than the conventional method.

PALANIAPPAN (1989) made a study on computers in education. He found that after introducing computers is schools for teaching, the attitude of teachers as well as students have changed. Many dull students scoreless through CAI, than the conventional method.

HEMALATHA (1989) studied on orientation of CAI. She concluded that the computers are commonly used in three main response sensitive strategies in CAI and suggested some levels of comparative involvement in decision making feature. They are drill and practice, tutorial and dialogue.

KARPAGA KUMARAVEL. R (1990) in his study on the effectiveness of computer assisted instruction video assisted instruction and conventional instruction in English language learning found that the achievement of video assisted instruction group in better than computer assisted instruction and conventional instructional group.

P. JEYAMANI (1991) pointed out that learning with computers offers a very powerful tool for educators and all efforts must be made to learners the potential of computers in education. This educational technology could therefore have a more on comparing role to play in the developing world. Thus the stimulation model of teaching through computer assisted instruction can readily be used for all types of teaching.

SARVANAN. M (1991) developed and validated a CAI package on X – rays for XI standard students. His findings revealed that the CAI packages were effective for individualized instruction.

PURUSHOTHAMAN and STELLA (1991) studied the effectiveness of CAI learning testing and guidance. The study reported that for low achievers self-testing and guidance through computer was found to be more effective.

BENEDICTO (1992) developed and validated a CAI packages on pollution for XI standard Biology students. The major findings of his study was learning the unit through CAI was faster for both slow and fast learners when compared with traditional teaching. He also reported the software developed ensures uniformity of achievement among Biology students.

MATHIVANAN (1994) attempted to develop and validate a CAI package on organisms an environment for IX standard pupils. His report revealed that the CAI package produced more significant effect on the achievement of the pupils of knowledge, comprehension, application and analysis level.

Dr. P. ANNARAJA and Smt. NIRMALA SUNDARARAJ (2005) made a study on power point presentation in teaching zoology pre post design was used in this that, they found that the power point presentation is effective in teaching zoology for higher secondary students.

JAYAKRUSHA CHOUDHARY (2005) conducted a study on effect of Computer Assisted Learning using method of enquiry in teaching physics in secondary school. Main objectives of this study was to test the efficiency of computer aided learning using method of inquiry in teaching physics at the secondary level on achievement and concept attainment. He found that CAI experimental method is to be more effective than conventional method of teaching.

G. SUBRAMANIAN (2006) pointed out major findings were computer assisted instruction significantly improves the performance of students, learning accountancy at higher secondary level. The combination of the colour, text, music and animation of the CAI package was well received by the students and the positive effect of same is perceptible from their achievement scores.

A computer factorial program on the laws and consents encountered in introductory physics courses among high school students was studied by EAUGHN AND KUHN (1979) these programmer were written with the weaker students in mind. But the researchers found that even stronger students used them presumably to check whether or not they really understood a particular phenomenon. This success was attributed to the fact that the programs were written so that each student's incorrect answer was dealt with in the novelty of using the computer encouraged students usage much more than the prospect of working from a study guide.

In another study, the efforts of CAI and reinforcement schedules on physics achievement towards physics of high school were measured by BANNET (1986). Seventy one high school students were taken as sample. The result of this study supported that students who received CAI would achieve significantly higher physics test scores. .

PASCUAL (1993) conducted a twofold study. He applied linguistics approach and empirical study designed to measure the degree of motivation in students learning English using CAI material and Non CAI material. He found that students belonging to CAI material showed more motivation than their counterparts.

SIEGLE (2000) the purpose of this study was to investigate whether exposure to multimedia and presentation software on laptop computers influenced student achievement in a secondary level anatomy and physiology science course. The study demonstrated that students learned more when they had access to laptop computers, were exposed to multimedia software, and created projects with presentation software.

VENDLINSKI et al (2002) conducted a quasi-experimental study with 134 first-year high school chemistry students using the Interactive Multimedia Exercises computer based learning and assessment tool to solve qualitative chemistry problems. Results of this study show a strong and significant correlation between computer aided measures of student understanding and the teacher's manual evaluation of student understanding using her own rubric.

SUSAN et al (2003) in his study examined 165 teachers' beliefs about student centered learning as they implemented Alien Rescue, a computer based programme for middle school science that was designed to create a Student Centered Learning Environment (SCLE) in the class room. Discusses the goal of student activity, the role of the teacher, assessment, and student interaction.

RABIA TABASSUM (2004) conducted a study on effect of Computer Assisted Instruction CAI on the Secondary School Students Achievement in Science. In his study analysis of data revealed that the class IX standard students taught through computer assisted instruction as supplementary strategy performed significantly better. The CAI was found equally effective for both male and female students.

WINTERS et al (2005) in this study 62 high school biology students, paired heterogeneously based on prior knowledge, learned about genetic using Gen Scope, a Computer Based Learning Environment. The results of this naturalistic study could potentially be used to inform educational practice by highlighting scaffolds that may foster self-regulated learning in a CBLE mediated science inquiry context.

HARSKAMP et al (2005) conducted a study on solving Physics Problems with the help of Computer Assisted Instruction" In this study the main goal of most Physics text books is to develop declarative and procedural knowledge exercises provide pupils with opportunities to apply this knowledge. The computer group taking part in the experiment did achieve higher results in solving problems.

CEPNI et al (2006) pointed out that the study on effects of Computer Assisted Instruction Material related to photosynthesis topic on student cognitive development misconceptions and attitudes. This study result showed that using CAIM in teaching photo synthesis topic was very effective for students to reach comprehension and application levels of cognitive domain.

MAHAMOOD FARHADIAN (2007) in his research, he studied the co-operative learning, Computer Assisted Instruction and combination of these two methods called Co-operative Computer Assisted Instruction (CCAI). In CCAI method with the use of computer and attractive software, there would be appropriate grounds in instruction and educational achievement of mathematics for students. This method was examined for small group of student in a workshop. He had investigated some hypotheses on reduce of the students negative beliefs about mathematics, the speed of learning mathematics and its independence from time scheduling. Findings of the study, the difference between pretest and posttest scores were meaningfully significant.

METHODOLOGY

Educational software development and validation is a major research and development activity in the field of education. The major area in educational software is occupied by the instructional software development. The nature and the impact of computer and learning were led to its acquiring more significance. In the latest concept of improvement in the instructional software produced and the role played by educational technologists in the consents and process of software development. The CAI package depends on the electronic device. Further there is need for the subject export, technical expert. Individualized instruction is the one-to-one relationship between learners and the subject to be learnt.

SELECTION OF AREA

The investigator has selected six schools in Udumalpet at Tiruppur District which come under the Tamil Nadu State Board of Education. The sample selected for study consists of boys and girls from rural and urban schools.

SELECTION OF THE SAMPLE

Sample selection is an important aspect of the research study, violation of a proper sampling method may yield based information of research and therefore maximum care is necessary for solution of sample.

English medium students of standard were selected from different types study the investigator selected three hundred students. Hundred and fifty boys and hundred and fifty girls of ninth standard from two government schools, two government aided schools and two unaided schools have been selected.

Considering the non-feasibility of formulating randomized groups in a school setting, it was decided to have purposive sampling as the method of sampling for this experiment. Hundred and fifty students of Class IX in each of the three type of schools were taken as CAI experimental group and hundred and fifty students of

Hundred and fifty students of Class IX in different types of rural schools and hundred and fifty students of Class IX in different types of urban schools were taken as the experimental group. The same schools are brought under the categories, group of different variables are follow. Purposive sampling procedure is applied for selecting the sampling and so that it is free from any prejudice. The following table presents the details of the samples selected for the study.

SAMPLING TECHNIQUE Pupils orzied and e samples selected for the study. e from any pre-judice.

For the present study purposive sampling method is used. The purposive sampling is selected by some arbitrary method because it is known to be representative of the total population. It is appropriate in a study which lays special emphasis on the control of certain specific variables.

DESIGN OF THE STUDY

The design selected for the study is the pretest and posttest of two groups.

1. Administrating a pretest measuring the dependent variable at initial stage for elimination of novelty factor.
2. Applying the treatment to the subject, to measure treatment effect.
3. Administering a posttest again for measuring the impact of the dependent variable.

Differences attributed to application of the experimental treatment are then determined by comparing pretest and posttest scores.

DEVELOPMENT OF INSTRUCTIONAL MATERIALS

The subject is to be converted into CAI package was "Circulatory System" in biology for IX standard students. The content frame work of the syllabus was adapted from the prescribed text by the Tamil Nadu State Board Text Book for IX standard. The teaching points were collected from the text books and other reference books mentioned and sequence according to the designed learning level of students in the local school. The content prescribed was corrected into a reading material in simple language according to their vocabulary level.

The teaching frames were structured on the learning materials following the norms and theories set for the preparation of CAI package. The teaching points were structured in small dosage called "Frame". Frames were arranged in proper sequence. In each frame information was presented with simple illustration or examples.

Objectives Starting Phase

Bloom's Taxonomy was used for objective formation specific behavioral objective was formulated as performance objectives on completion of learning the unit "Circulatory System" the student should be able to identify. Content analysis was done. Care was taken to link the content by appropriate sequencing strategy.

1. Define "Blood"
2. State the composition of blood
3. Name the types of blood
4. List the properties of blood
5. Distinguish RBC, WBC and Platelet
6. Describe the functions of blood and
7. Define "Blood Group"

DESCRIPTION OF THE TOOL USED

a) Computer Assisted Instruction Package : The instructional soft ware package developed to help the learners through a prescribed form of self instruction the subject are to be converted into frame. In this study in biology CAI package was Circulatory System for IX standard students. This CAI package contains various stimuli such as showing pictures and animation. This CAI was an instructional effective material individualized.

b) Performa Sheet : The investigator herself has developed a Performa sheet to collect necessary information regarding the individuals back ground such as the name, age, sex, name and address of the school, locality, type of school, system of school.

c) Science Achievement Test : In this present study the investigator was prepared the achievement test question paper based on the IX standard State Board Syllabus. The question has been given to IX students of the selected school situated in and around Coimbatore. In consists of 40 questions and each objective has been provided 4 multiple choice from which the individual is asked to mark the response which he/she feels to be right in their point of view.

d) Scoring Key: The answer scripts for the conducted achievement test were collected and scored based on the scoring key. The score the test it was decided to give one mark as weightage for each correct answer. Thus a maximum of 40 marks who give correct response for all the items.

JURY OPINION

The copies of achievement test were submitted to a group of five subject experts who are teachers in schools and colleges for their valuable suggestion. Based on their ideas, the structure of questions was modified, options of some questions were changed and the number of question was also increased. They were asked to examine whether the items fully covered the content of "Circulating System" presented for IX standard by Tamil Nadu Text-book society. Items which were choose or similar or deviant was dropped as recommended by experts. They items reflected the entire context. Thus the context validity of the test was established based on expert judgments. As a result the test tool for the final study was prepared with forty multiple choice questions.

PILOT STUDY

Pilot study is a vital factor is any research. The pilot study administered to 50 student of IX standard level.

ADMINISTRATION OF TOOL

The study was conducted and materials were distributed to the students after taking prior permission from the head master of the selected schools. The investigator personally visited each school and collected the data. The purpose and intention of the study were briefly explained. The subjects had been repeatedly assured that they could freely express their opinions without and reservation since the purpose was purely educational research. The co-operation extended by the respondents/students was encouraging remarkable.

METHODS OF EXPERIMENTATION

Each sample was pre-tested with criteria referenced test to measure the entry level. Before the experiment or treatment the students were pre-tested using the test. The test was helpful in accessing subject knowledge of the students prior to treatment. The same test was administered again after treatment effects. The individual instruction analysis was carried by employing't' test for difference between the CAI groups.

DATA COLLECTION

As presented pre test, post test was planned to achieve the objective of the study. The sample was selected for conducting the experiment. For conducting the experiment the investigator selected six Higher Secondary School, The investigator selected Higher Secondary School hence it would be easy to provide the treatment in the school to the sample.

STATISTICAL TECHNIQUES USED IN THE STUDY

Appropriate statistical techniques were used which included the mean, standard deviation, t-test and ANOVA.

ANALYSIS AND INERPRETATION OF THE DATA COMPUTATION OF STATISTICS

The first section deals with background information of the selected sample based on age, gender, type of school, educational status of parents, and socio-economic status of the family.

In second section the scores of pre test and post test were calculated and the statistical techniques like mean, standard deviation, t-test and ANOVA were used for analyzing and interpreting. Descriptive analysis for Background information of the selected sample

DIFFERENTIAL ANALYSIS

The collected data were consolidated, tabulated and analysed statistically by using the following tests.

1. Test of Significance ('t' Test and ANOVA)
2. Mean and Standard Deviation

(1) Test of significance: 't' Test and ANOVA

't' Test is used to find out the significant level of difference between two groups of population. The values are calculated with the help of the mean scores and standard deviation.

(2) Mean and Standard Deviation

Mean and standard deviation were done using the results of the study to make simple comparisons wherever necessary.

ANALYSIS OF 't' TEST SCORES OF GOVERNMENT SCHOOLS PUPIL FOLLOWING THE COMPUTER ASSISTED INSTRUCTION

Source	N	Mean	Standard Deviation	't' value
Pre test Score	50	14.300	3.2467	34.799 **
Post test Score	50	32.22	3.3030	

** Significant at 1% level.

There is no significant difference between the pretest and posttest scores of Government schools pupil following the Computer Assisted Instruction was rejected.

ANALYSIS OF 't' TEST SCORES OF AIDED SCHOOLS PUPIL FOLLOWING THE COMPUTER ASSISTED INSTRUCTION

Source	N	Mean	Standard Deviation	't' value
Pre test Score	50	15.44	4.6342	22.206 **
Post test Score	50	29.76	4.3451	

** Significant at one percent level.

There is no significant difference between the pretest and posttest scores of Aided Schools Pupil following the Computer Assisted Instruction was rejected.

ANALYSIS OF 't' TEST SCORES OF UNAIDED SCHOOLS PUPIL FOLLOWING THE COMPUTER ASSISTED INSTRUCTION

Source	N	Mean	Standard Deviation	't' value
Pre test Score	50	13.16	3.6048	33.969 **
Post test Score	50	28.98	3.1975	

** Significant at 1% level.

There is no significant difference between the pretest and posttest scores of Unaided Schools Pupil following the Computer Assisted Instruction was rejected.

SIGNIFICANCE OF DIFFERENCE BETWEEN PRE AND POST TESTS SCORES OF COMPUTER ASSISTED INSTRUCTION GROUP

Test	N	Mean	Standard Deviation	't' value
Pre test	150	14.30	3.9591	47.644 **
Post test	150	30.32	3.8831	

** Significant at 1% level.

There is no significant difference between the pretest and posttest mean scores of the experimental group following CAI was rejected.

COMPARISON OF POSTTEST PERFORMANCE OF COMPUTER ASSISTED INSTRUCTION GROUP BETWEEN THE DIFFERENT TYPE OF SCHOOLS

Type of the School	N	Mean	Standard Deviation	'F' value
Government School	50	32.22	3.3030	12.824 **
Aided School	50	29.76	4.6451	
Unaided School	50	30.32	3.1975	

** Significant at 1% level.

ANOVA test was applied and the calculated ANOVA value is 12.824, which is found to be significant at 0.01% level. There is no significant difference in posttest performance of Computer Assisted Instruction between the different types of schools pupil was rejected.

COMPARISON OF THE POST TEST PERFORMANCE OF THE EXPERIMENTAL GROUP FOLLOWING THE CAI WITH REFERENCE TO LOCALITY TABLE - 24

Area	N	Mean	Standard Deviation	't' value
Urban	75	32.00	3.2715	5.862 **
Rural	75	28.64	3.7331	

** Significant at 1% level.

There is no significance difference between posttest performance of Urban and Rural Schools Pupil following the Computer Assisted Instruction was rejected.

COMPARISON OF THE POSTTEST PERFORMANCE OF THE EXPERIMENTAL GROUP FOLLOWING THE CAI WITH REFERENCE TO GENDER

Gender	N	Mean	Standard Deviation	t' value'
Boys	75	29.6667	4.0415	** 2.084
Girls	75	30.9733	3.6279	

** Significant at 5% level.

There is no significance difference between the posttest performance of Boys and Girls following Computer Assisted Instruction was rejected.

SUMMARY AND CONCLUSION

SUMMARY OF THE STUDY

The study is an attempt to find out, a comparative study of effectiveness of Computer Assisted Instruction and Handout Instruction on circulatory system for IX standard students.

A sample of 300 pupils studying in IX standard from six different schools in Udumalpet Taluk, Coimbatore District was selected. 150 formed of the 300 students experimental group following Computer Assisted Instruction. The experimental method was adopted in the study. Achievement test question paper was employed as a tool, at this time the treatment is administered on a small group of the target population. Pretest and post test are administered prior to starting and after the completion of the treatment respectively. The test scores were taken to assess the effectiveness of self learning through the Computer Assisted Instruction among students.

FINDINGS OF STUDY

1. The comparison of scores of pretest and post test of Government Schools Pupil following the Computer Assisted Instruction shows significant difference. The mean posttest scores is 32.22 for the Government Schools Pupil which is greater than pretest scores 14.30. This shows the Computer Assisted Instruction significantly influenced learning of pupil.
2. The mean posttest scores is 29.79 for the Aided Schools Pupil which is greater than pretest scores 15.44. This shows the CAI significantly influenced the learning of Aided Schools Pupil.
3. The mean posttest scores is 28.98 for unaided schools pupil which is higher than mean pretest scores 13.16. This shows the CAI significantly influenced the learning of unaided schools pupil.
4. The comparison of the scores of pretest and posttest of overall sample in target group following Computer Assisted instruction shows significant difference. This mean posttest scores is 30.32 for samples which is greater than the mean pretest scores 14.32. This shows CAI significantly influenced learning of all selected samples following CAI.
5. In this study it was found that same Government Schools has also showing better performance, while they received experimental treatment through CAI when compared to unaided schools and aided schools respectively in post test score.
6. The comparison of the posttest scores of urban and rural area in the CAI experimental group shows significant difference, the mean value of this CAI experimental group is 32.00 and 28.64 respectively.
7. Gender wise comparison in the CAI experimental group proved the significant. The calculated 't' value is 2.084. The mean scores of girls are 30.97, which is greater than the mean scores of boys 29.66 in the posttest performances.

RECOMMENDATION

1. Computer assisted instruction should be implemented in more number of the schools.
2. The Government should allot more funds to provide adequate number of computer materials for the schools.
3. It is recommended that Government may give concession for purchase of computer.

4. College students who are studying computer science may be asked to do projects in the development of necessary software for high school syllabus. This can solve the problem of non availability of software.
5. Special training shall be given to the teachers through in-service training programme to inculcate knowledge about different instructional strategies.
6. Educational institutions should have adequate instructional materials.
7. Training shall be given to the teachers to prepare and handle instrumental materials.
8. Instruction materials of learning provide scope for self instructional activities. Here the role of the teacher is limited and maximum activities are prescribed to the learners.
9. Teacher can improve their competence by attending in service training camps and also by writing research articles in the field of educational technology.
10. The students can learn effectively when they learn on their own. Self learning develops critical thinking in handling of study materials on one's own and enhances communication skills and self reliance.
11. The teachers must motivate the pupils to make more instructional package for self learning.

SUGGESTIONS FOR FURTHER RESEARCH

A Research study would be incomplete if it doesn't provide necessary guidelines as well as potential research topics for further exploration. The following suggestions are made for further research in this area.

1. A similar study can be carried out in different types of school in different parts of Tamil Nadu.
2. In the present study researcher didn't take students from Tamil medium high schools students from such schools can be taken for further study.

CONCLUSION

The density of the country is destined in the classroom. Yes, it is true. The education has a wider meaning now-a-days. The education in the present trend does not mean the mere text book learning. It aims at giving complete life to the pupils. It is more important for the learners to know how to learn rather than what to learn.

From the results of the study, the investigator has ideas of Computer Assisted Instruction provided greater learning opportunities for children both theoretical and practical. Its use in bringing new kinds of experiences for children in school is really interesting and meaningful. The investigator therefore desires that the more number of educational institutions should come forward to make the learning best out of all available instruction materials for learning. So, this amount is just the beginning... not the end.

REFERENCES

1. Aggarwal J.G (1995), Essential of Educational Technology; Teaching Leaning Innovations in Education New Delhi.
2. Bloom, Benjamin S (1956), Taxonomy of Educational Objective Hand books. The cognitive domain. Logmas Publication, New York.
3. Chauhan S.S (1983), Innovations in Teaching Learning Process, New Delhi. Coulson S.E (1962), Programmed Learning and Computer based instruction.
4. Forcier (2000) The Computer as a Productivity Tool in Education, Prentice Hall of India.Glass G.V (1970), Statistical method in Education and Psychology, Prentice Hall, Englewood Cliffs.
5. S.P.Gupta (1985), Statistic methods Sultan Chand & Sons Pub. New Delhi. Pp930.
6. John Best. W (1963), Research in Education Prentice Hall of India Private Limited, New Delhi.
7. Krishnamoorthy. R (1995) Computer Programming, JJ Publishers, Madurai.
8. Kulkarni S.(1986), Introduction to Educational Technology, New Delhi. Oxford,IBH Pub. Co.,
9. Mangal S.K (2000), Reversed Edition Foundation of Education Technology.
10. Murthy S.K (1995), Educational Technology Parkash Brothers, Jallandhar.
11. Narayana L.M, A text book of Chordates, Saras Publication, Nagercoil.
12. Pillay, Subramania G (1995), Readings in Educational Technology, Nirmal Publication, Madurai.
13. Rajaraman, (1985), Fundamentals of Computer, New Delhi, Prentice Hall of India Pvt. Ltd.,
14. Sadha and Singh (1982) Methodology of Educational Research, Prentice Hall of India.
15. Sampath and Pannerselvam (1994), Introduction to Educational Technology, Sterling Publishers, New Delhi.
16. Satyanarayana (1985), Research Methodology, Methods and Techniques, Atlantic Pub.
17. Vachan Sing (2005), Practical Approach Educational Technology, Akansha Publishing House, New Delhi.
18. Venkataian (2000), Encylopedio of Contemporary Education Series Science Education, Anmol Pub.
19. Yadav (2000), Modern method of teaching sciences, Anmol Publisher, Delhi.
20. Zaidi (2004), Modern method of teaching Science, Anmol Publisher, New Delhi.

❐

16.

Utilization of E-Resources among B.Ed Students

INDRODUCTION

An "electronic resource" is defined as any work encoded and made available for access through the use of a computer. It includes electronic data available by (1) remote access and (2) direct access (fixed media). In other words: Remote access (electronic resources) refers to the use of electronic resources via computer networks. Direct Access (electronic resources) refers to the use of electronic resources via carriers (e.g., discs/disks, cassettes, cartridges) designed to be inserted into a computerized device or its auxiliary equipment.

NEED AND SIGNIFIGANCE OF THE STUDY

Now we are in the age of knowledge explosion. Teaching-learning process changed from teacher centered to student centered. It is true that the learning process is optimum when it is assisted and personalized. Technology Enhanced learning (TEL) plays an important role in personalizing the learning process. Thus knowing about E-Resources and its utilization is very important for B.Ed., students. Hence investigator has taken the following topic for her investigation.

TITLE OF THE PROBLEM

The problem undertaken by the investigator is "Utilization of E-Resources among B.Ed., Students".

DEFINITION OF TERMS

Utilization

Means the act of using Refers hear using the Electronic Resources such as E-Learning, E-Tutoring, E-Books, E-Banking and E-Shopping.

E-Resources

Refers to Electronic Resources such as E-Learning, E-Tutoring, E-Books, E-Library, E-Banking and E-Shopping.

B.Ed., Students

This refers to the students studying B.Ed., in the colleges of education.

OBJECTIVES OF THE STUDY

1. To find out the level of utilization of E-Resources and its dimensions among B.Ed., students with respect to total number of students.
2. To find out the level of utilization of E-Resources and its dimensions among B.Ed., students with respect to gender.
3. To find out the level of utilization of E-Resources and its dimensions among B.Ed., students with respect to religion.

NULL HYPOTHESIS OF THE STUDY

1. There is no significant difference between male and female B.Ed., students in their utilization of e-resources and its dimensions.
2. There is no significant difference between rural and urban B.Ed., colleges in their utilization of e-resources and its dimensions.
3. There is no significant difference between day-scholar and hosteller B.Ed., students in their utilization of e-resources and its dimensions.

DELIMITATIONS OF THE STUDY

1. The sample of the study is limited to only Seven B.Ed College students.
2. The present investigation is confined only to B.Ed students.
3. The present study included only 6 dimensions of e-resources.
4. The present study is limited to Tirunelveli district only.
5. Sample for study is limited to 300 B.Ed students.

METHOD USED IN THE STUDY

The Investigator used survey method for the study.

POPULATION FOR THE STUDY

The population of the study includes the students of B.Ed., courses in Tirunelveli district.

SAMPLE OF THE STUDY

The investigator has used simple random sampling technique for selecting the colleges under Tamil Nadu Teacher's Education University, Chennai. The investigator selected the B.Ed., colleges in Tirunelveli District. Investigator selected 300 B.Ed. students from 9 colleges in this district, giving importance to gender and location of college.

TOOLS USED IN THE PRESENT STUDY

Utilization of e-resources scale developed and validated by the investigator with the help of guide.

STATISTICAL TECHNIQUES USED IN THE PRESENT STUDY

The Investigator has used the following statistical techniques

1. Percentage Analysis
2. Arithmetic Mean
3. Standard Deviation
4. 't' test
5. Anova

Hypothesis: 1

There is no significant difference between rural and urban B.Ed students in their utilization of e-resources and its dimensions.

Significant difference between Rural and Urban College Students in their Utilization of e-resources among B.Ed. students

Dimensions	Locality of the College	N	Mean	Std. Deviation	't' Value	Remarks
D1 e-learning	Rural	188	41.98	5.436	3.31	S
	Urban	112	44.09	5.174		
D2 e-tutoring	Rural	188	22.69	3.344	1.26	NS
	Urban	112	23.20	3.448		
D3 e-books	Rural	188	29.49	4.641	2.42	S
	Urban	112	30.77	4.020		
D4 e-library	Rural	188	14.73	2.751	1.59	NS
	Urban	112	15.24	2.593		
D5 e-banking	Rural	188	18.52	3.331	1.55	NS
	Urban	112	19.15	3.529		
D6 e-shopping	Rural	188	17.31	3.907	0.42	NS
	Urban	112	17.50	3.293		
Utilization of e-resources	Rural	188	144.72	17.173	2.55	S
	Urban	112	149.95	17.037		

At 5% level of significance the table value of 't' is 1.96

It is inferred from the above table that there is significant difference between rural and urban college students in the utilization of e-resources among B.Ed students.

Hypothesis: 2

There is no significant difference between Hindu, Christian and Muslim B.Ed students in their utilization of e-resources and its dimensions.

RELIGION

Significant difference among Hindu, Christian and Muslim Students in their utilization of e-resources among B.Ed. students.

Dimensions	Source of Variation	Sum of Squares	df	Mean Square	F Value
D1 e-learning	Between Groups	396.245	2	198.123	6.994
	Within Groups	8413.421	297	28.328	
	Total	8809.667	299		
D2 e-tutoring	Between Groups	212.816	2	106.408	9.828
	Within Groups	3215.621	297	10.827	
	Total	3428.437	299		
D3 e-books	Between Groups	201.968	2	100.984	5.231
	Within Groups	5733.699	297	19.305	
	Total	5935.667	299		
D4 e-library	Between Groups	51.960	2	25.980	3.626
	Within Groups	2128.120	297	7.165	
	Total	2180.080	299		
D5 e-banking	Between Groups	144.240	2	72.120	6.411
	Within Groups	3340.997	297	11.249	
	Total	3485.237	299		
D6 e-shopping	Between Groups	72.599	2	36.300	2.703
	Within Groups	3988.318	297	13.429	
	Total	4060.917	299		
Utilization of e-resources	Between Groups	5380.714	2	2690.357	9.523
	Within Groups	83903.616	297	282.504	
	Total	89284.330	299		

At 5% level of significance, for (2,297) df the table value of 'F' is 3.03

CONCLUSION

From the above study, the utilization of e-resources among B.Ed.,students is average and can be improved. This should be improved through the proper designing of curriculum and providing proper facilities for utilization of e-resources.

❐

17.

Effectiveness of Edu-Digital Skill among Higher Secondary Students in Coimbatore District

INTRODUCTION

The end of the 20th Century and beginning of the 21st Century witnessed very exciting changes, one of them being in the field of Information and Communication Technology. Educators have begin to realize that in the fast changing world of today, the students have to be prepared to cope intelligently with the social, economic and technological changes. The educational environment is changing rapidly as a consequence of ICT and will continue to change. Information and Communication Technologies (ICT) are electronic and/or computerized devices and associated human interactive materials that enable the user to employ them for a wide range of teaching and learning processes in addition to personal use. Around the world, educational systems are under increasing pressure to use the new information and communication technologies to teach students the knowledge and skills they need in the 21st Century. With the emerging new technologies, the teaching profession is evolving from an emphasis on teacher-centered, lecture-based instruction to student-centered, interactive learning environments. The present study aims to find out the effectiveness of edu-digital skill among higher secondary students in Coimbatore District. A samples of 100 higher secondary students selected randomly were studied. A questionnaire method of survey was used to find out the effectiveness of edu-digital skill higher secondary students. The data were collected by using questionnaire as an instrument. Primary data were collected by conducting direct structured interview using questionnaire. All the respondents were asked the same questions in the same fashion and they were informed the purpose of study. t-test, Regression and correlation analysis were applied to test the hypotheses. The findings and observations are the result and outcome of the interpretations made during the study of analysis. The result found that edu-digital skill are positively correlated with higher secondary students.

Education, the foremost weapon for social reform, is now under the forces of change. Newly formed branches of knowledge and techniques of education facilitate the physical, mental and emotional development of the learners. Schools have an unavoidable role in acquainting the students with the nature of changing field of education and in making necessary changes in the instructional techniques. In the modern world of technological innovations, all educational institutions are trying to improve their quality in terms of facilities and academic outputs.

Scientific knowledge is exploding every day. Knowledge available to mankind today is emerging in the form of science and technology. There is no limit or end to the accumulation of scientific knowledge. It also satisfies the intellectual thirst of human beings. Science education is a bridge between science and education, using psychology. It links the most powerful concepts of science to the growing minds of children through active experimental pedagogy. Science education plays a prominent role in Indian educational system. It has, as its objective, the aim of providing individual learners a firm grasp of the concepts and processes of science as also to impart the ability to use scientific method of problem-solving. As a result of it, every aspect of human civilization has been influenced to a very great extent.

The present world is the world of science and technology. Science is the most inexhaustible storehouse of knowledge. Continuous advances in scientific and technological research have led to the growth and greater application of science in contemporary society. The purpose of science education is to give individuals a firm grasps of the concepts and processes of science and to develop scientific attitude, scientific reasoning, problem solving ability and scientific temper and to impart them the ability to use the scientific method to other situations in life. Hence science education has been included in school curriculum at all levels. It is however necessary that science teaching be impressive so as to inculcate its values in young minds.

The increasing importance of informatics in day-to-day life has resulted in the emergence of computers in education at the international level. The worldwide recognition gained for the importance of computers has compelled educationists to revise the existing curricula to include informatics components. Even the developing countries have realized that unless they invest heavily in computer education, they will be left behind in the informatics revolution. Computers are being used in education to prepare the children for the informatics future by training them in programming and related skills for work in the informatics industry. They are also being used as educational aids to improve children's skills in academic subjects at all levels of education. Introduction of computers in education has brought out changes in the content and methods of education. However, lack of resources remains one of the main obstacles to the introduction and development of informatics in education in a large way in developing countries.

The most striking innovation in the field of educational technology is the use of computers. Computer is included in the hardware approach of educational technology. It is one of the machines of automation in teaching and learning and is used for presenting individualized instruction. The main objective of teaching through computer is to provide the needed flexibility for individualizing the educational process. It meets the specific needs of the student in a way in which is almost impossible to do in a face-to face student-teacher relationship.

Computers should have a major role in the teaching-learning process. Computers have become an essential class room tool for the acquisition, analysis, presentation, and communication of data in ways that allow students to become active participants in research and learning. The computers offer students very important resources for learning concepts through simulations, graphics, sound, data manipulation and model building. Computers can improve scientific learning and facilitate communication of ideas and concepts.

There are three roles for computer in education. First, it functions as a tutor for students by presenting material, evaluating responses, and depending on the basis of the evaluation, deciding what to present next. Second, it is a tool that helps students perform calculations, analyze data, keep records, or write papers. Third, it functions as tutee by having told what to do through programming.

A computer program can be designed to create models for experimental purpose. Students, that particularly in higher education, have the benefits of using computer as a computational tool. They learn a programming language and write a program to solve some of their course work problems treating the computer as an aid in much the same way as a slide rule or a set of mathematical tables. Computers are capable of giving almost instant feedback, tirelessly, no matter how many learners 'get it wrong' and it is equally well known that human tutors have limited value when it comes to learners repeatedly getting things wrong.

REVIEW OF LITERATURE

Dalacosta et al. (2009) developed and studied the effectiveness of Multimedia **application with animated cartoons in teaching science in elementary education.** The results of the study provide evidence that the use of animated cartoons significantly increases the young students' knowledge and understanding of specific science concepts, which are normally difficult to comprehend and often cause misconceptions to them.

Jian Hu et al. (2009) investigated the effects of introducing a software program, named the Dental 3D Multimedia System (D3DM), into the education of a group of junior dental students in their preclinical practice. One group received their training program in the traditional way, unassisted by 3D technology. The second group received their training program in the traditional manner, but also used the D3DM to supplement their education. The results showed that the

D3DM-assisted group achieved higher scores and also indicated that the usage of 3D multimedia PC software had a positive impact on several aspects of subjects' performance.

Kanmani and Radha (2009) studied the Effectiveness of CAI package in basic electronics teaching. There was a significant difference between the control and the experimental group students in attainment of knowledge level, understanding level, and application level objective in the gain scores. Hence, the experimental group students were better than the control group students in attainment of knowledge level, understanding level, and application level objective in the gain scores. It was inferred from the finding that the experimental treatment is effective to the students.

Korakakis et al. (2009) made a study on the "**3D visualization types in multimedia applications for science learning for 8th grade students in Greece".** The aim of the study was to determine whether the use of specific types of visualization (3D illustration, 3D animation, and interactive 3D animation) combined with narration and text, contributes to the learning process in science courses. The results indicated that multimedia applications with interactive 3D animations as well as with 3D animations do in fact increase the interest of students and make the material more appealing to them.

She, Hsiao-Ching and Chen, Yi-Zen (2009) examined how middle school students constructed their understanding of the mitosis and meiosis processes at a molecular level through multimedia learning materials presented in different interaction and sensory modality modes. The dependent variables included subjects' pre-test, post-test, and retention-test scores, showing their understanding of mitosis and meiosis process at molecular level. The results of the study showed that the group which used multimedia learning material has a greater amount of visual attention and consistent with their long term retained learning than the group which did not use the same. This study adds empirical evidence of a direct correlation between the length of eye fixation behavior and the depth of learning. Moreover, it provides insight into the multimedia effect on students' cognitive process through the use of eye fixation behavior evidence.

Anboucarassy (2010) studied the effectiveness of Multimedia in Teaching Biological Science to IX Standard students. The results of the study revealed that experiment group performed better than the control group due to the exposure of multimedia based learning. Thus multimedia helps the students to sustain their interest and also their retention power compared to the traditional method of teaching. The constant use of multimedia will make students understand more and achieve more in their academic achievement. Hence it was concluded that the multimedia approach is considered to be one of the best techniques for biology teaching at IX standard level.

Ponraj and Sivakumar (2010) studied the effectiveness of Computer-Assisted Instruction in Teaching Zoology in Relation to Learners' Personality.

The major findings of the study indicated that achievement scores of experimental group students were higher than the control group students after the treatment.

Yusuf, Mudasiru and Afolabi, Adedeji (2010) investigated the effects of computer assisted instruction (CAI) on secondary school students' performance in biology. The findings of the study showed that the performance of students exposed to CAI either individually or cooperatively were better than their counterparts exposed to the conventional classroom instruction. Based on the research findings recommendations were made on the need to develop relevant CAI packages for teaching biology in Nigerian secondary schools.

OBJECTIVES

1. To know the edu-digital skill among higher secondary students in Coimbatore district.
2. To find out the effectiveness of Multimedia Programme in teaching among higher secondary students.

METHODOLOGY

Research may be termed as a systemic inquiry of verified knowledge, it is an organized deliberate effort to collect information, to analyze it, to put it together and finally to evaluate it. This research paper on methodology describes elaborately, the sample that was chosen, research design, objectives of the study, data collection, statistical techniques used for data and analysis.

Population

Population selected for this study was 100 higher secondary students in a selected school at Coimbatore District.

Attitude Scale towards Multimedia Programme

The attitude scale was used to measure the level of attitude towards Multimedia programme. The scale was constructed and validated by the investigator.

The attitude scale towards multimedia programme, consisting of 40 items, was designed by the investigator and was given to experienced teachers who were handling Computer Science in higher secondary schools, professors of Computer Science and Education and Educational psychologists. On the basis of the suggestions of above experts, some items were restructured and some were eliminated. Finally 25 items were selected for this test. The scale for measuring the higher secondary student's attitude towards multimedia programme in the study is of the Likert type. This scale has as many as 25 statements of which 20 are favourable towards multimedia programme and the remaining are unfavourable towards it.

Scoring

In the Likert type of scale, against each statement, five alternatives namely "Strongly agree", "Agree", "Undecided", "Disagree", and "Strongly disagree" are given. The subjects have to indicate their choice by putting a tick-mark (√) under one of the five columns against each statement.

For favourable statement weightage of 4,3,2,1 and 0 were given from strongly agree to strongly disagree in that order. For unfavourable statements the scoring was reversed. Thus the strongly agree response will get 0 and the strongly disagree response will get 4. Here the weight age of 0,1,2,3 and 4 were given from strongly agree to the strongly disagree in that order.

Thus the score value lies between 0-100. The content validity of the tool was established based on the opinion given by the experts. The reliability of the tool was established by Split-Half method. It was found to be 0.83 which was significant.

Data Collection

Primary data, required for the present research work were collected by conducting direct interviews using questionnaire. All the respondents were given sufficient information about the Project work. These respondents were provided with the same questionnaires. They were also informed that they have to answer in the same fashion.

HYPOTHESIS

There is no significant difference between the pre and post test mean scores of experimental group students in their attitude towards multimedia programme.

Administration of retention test

The Attitude Scale towards Multimedia Programme was constructed and validated by the investigator and was administered to the subjects of the experimental group. The pre test scores on attitude towards multimedia programme were collected. Thus pre test and post test scores on attitude towards multimedia programme were computed for analysis.

ANALYSIS AND INTERPRETATION

To find out the significance of the difference between the pre and post test mean scores of experimental group students in their attitude towards multimedia programme the 't' test was used.

Table 1: Distribution of 't' value between the pre and post test mean scores of experimental group students in their attitude towards multimedia programme

Group	N	Mean	S.D	't' value	Level of Significant
Pre test	50	42.08	10.42	24.47	$p<0.05$
Post test	50	93.58	2.57		

There is no significant difference between the pre and post test mean scores of experimental group students in their attitude towards multimedia programme.

The obtained 't' value is statistically significant since it is greater than the table 't' value 1.96 at 0.05 level of significance. Hence the null hypothesis is rejected. It shows that there is significant difference between the pre and post test mean scores of experimental group students in their attitude towards multimedia programme. It is therefore concluded that the experimental group students show more favourable attitude towards multimedia programme in the post test than the pre test.

Table 2: Showing the Stepwise regression analysis predicting factors influencing effectiveness of edu-digital skill among higher secondary students and demographic variables

Sl.No	Step/Source	Unstandardized Coefficients Beta	Std. Error	Standardized Coefficients Beta Beta	Step t	P
1.	Gender	1.144	0.156	0.242	7.324	0.01
2.	Father education	1.254	0.359	0.163	3.495	0.01
3.	Mother education	2.615	0.462	0.361	5.661	0.01
4.	Monthly Income	2.175	0.402	0.280	5.410	0.01
5.	Father Occupation	1.022	0.513	0.137	1.992	0.01

P < 0.01 *

Five variables viz Gender, Father education, Mother education, Monthly income and Father Occupation have significantly contributed for predicting the factors influencing effectiveness of edu-digital skill among higher secondary. The first variable Gender seems to be 7.324, Father education seems to be 3.495, Mother education seems to be 5.661, Monthly income seems to be 5.410 and Father occupation seems to be 1.992. The predictive value of these variables separately is 0.01.

Table 3: Showing the correlation between the effectiveness of edu-digital skill among higher secondary students and demographic variables

Factors	Effectiveness of edu-digital skill among higher secondary students
Gender	0.920**
Father education	0.849**
Mother education	0.914**
Monthly Income	0.880**
Father Occupation	0.855**

* Significant at 0.01 level

Effectiveness of edu-digital skill among higher secondary students is positively and significantly related to Gender (0.920), Father education (0.849), Mother education (0.914), Monthly income (0.880) and Father occupation (0.855). So, the direct relationship between the effectiveness of edu-digital skill among higher secondary students and selected demographic variables.

CONCLUSION

Computer and multimedia technology for education offers a number of benefits. They allow the teacher to structure and present the information with varying special effects to the students. They can also be used for the storage of audio-visual information of various types. Multimedia programmes provide a lot of benefits. The benefits for learners include flexibility of scheduled instruction at a location convenient to learners, reduced student time, assured progress in skill development, increased achievement and increased retention and continuous report to the learners of progress and accomplishments, specified performance criteria, good response and feedback.

The application of multimedia programme would definitely create a good learning environment in classroom, sustaining attention and motivating the students to learn effectively. The application of multimedia may create a congenial learning climate in schools and can bring real life situations.

The investigator has chosen the topic for the present study in order to address the problem faced by teachers, teaching science, to foster involvement in new teaching approaches, to get a feeling of satisfaction through learning in the classroom, to create joyful learning environment and to stimulate active information processing for effective learning,

In a vast country like India, enormous work is now being done in the field of education, but it is still not possible to equip each and every school with all the facilities for teaching science. Secondary schools need high quality teaching aids. Multimedia, as a teaching aid, is very much effective with colour, sound and graphics, which are found in the audio, video movie media. Any diagram can be explained in detail with 3D effects, which helps the students understand clearly. The students can get a live vision of life's aspects and scientific factors. Multimedia includes use of computer.

The present study has found out that the multimedia programme is very effective in higher secondary level. As the present teaching-learning process in higher secondary classes is very rigid, time bound and outmoded, it was proposed to use multimedia programme.

As multimedia programme develops a favourable attitude towards multimedia programme, motivates the students to involve in the process of learning, attracts students' attention in learning, accelerates the students' understanding of concepts of subjects, increases the retention power and that it is highly suitable for all categories of students ranging from low to high achievers, it is suggested that this multimedia programme be widely adopted and implemented in educational institutions as computer laboratory facilities are available in all the schools and colleges to enable the learners to learn the subjects of their choice according to their own pace and ability. Learning through multimedia programme is very easy, understandable and comfortable to all categories of students for all types of subjects.

REFERENCES

1. Anboucarassy, B. (2010). Effectiveness of Multimedia in Teaching Biological Science to IX Standard students. EDUTRACKS, 9(5): 37-38.
2. Dalacosta, K., Kamariotaki-Paparrigopoulou, M., Palyvos, J.A., & Spyrellis, N. (2009). Multimedia application with animated cartoons for teaching science in elementary education. Computers & Education, 52(4): 741-748.
3. Jian Hu, Hao Yu, Jun Shao, Zhiyong Li, Jiawei Wang & Yining Wang (2009). Effects of dental 3D multimedia system on the performance of junior dental students in preclinical practice: a report from China. Advances in Health Sciences Education, 14(1): 123-133.
4. Kanmani, M., & Radha, M. (2009). "Effectiveness of CAI package in basic electronics teaching", Journal of All India Association for Educational Research, 21(1): 47-50.
5. Korakakis, G., Pavlatou, E.A., Palyvos, J. A., & Spyrellis N. (2009). 3D visualization types in multimedia applications for science learning: A case study for 8th grade students in Greece. Computers & Education, 52(2): 390-401.
6. Ponraj, P., & Sivakumar, R. (2010). Computer-Assisted Instruction in Zoology in Relation to Learners' Personality. EDUTRACKS, 9(6): 34-37.
7. Yusuf, Mudasiru O., & Afolabi, Adedeji O. (2010). Effects of Computer AssistedIinstruction (CAI) on Secondary School students' performance in biology. TOJET: The Turkish Online Journal of Educational Technology, 9(1): 62-69.

❐

18.

Effectiveness of Educational Software on Achievement in Chemistry among Students of Standard XI

INTRODUCTION

Computer Assisted Instruction (CAI) has emerged as an effective and efficient media of instruction in the advanced countries of the world. CAI is being used in the formal and non – formal educations at all levels. In India too computer has been introduced in most of the areas such as data processing, decision making, etc., It has impact on the working methods of research and development in the field of Science and Technology. First CAI attempt was made around 1961 when University of Illinois produced Programmed Logic for Automatic Teaching Operation (PLATO). Hence, the use of computer in general education started from early sixties. The Computer Assisted or Aided Instruction may be defined as the use of computer as an integral part of an instructional system, the learner generally engaging in two – way interaction with the computer via terminal.

"Designate', is a Educational Software developed by Eureka Educational Software which is a 17 years old Multimedia Production House, involved into various activities like making of interactive presentation, animated films, music videos, special effects. They are the first people in India to do a full four minute animated music video where a live character interacts and dance with a computer generated character Anaida's " Hoo Halla Hoo". They received an award for Best Animation from Autodesk. Eureka Educational Software developed 'Designmate', which were converting the entire textbooks into colourful 3D animated movies with interactive games and puzzles. Bringing a visually beautiful and interesting learning experience, enhancing the student's learning and retention capabilities. This Education Software was distributed to Schools via Server and LAN. This Education Software covers Science and Mathematics subjects from class VI to XII.

Objectives of the Study

The objectives of the study are:

1. To find out the significant difference between the Pre – Test Scores of the Control and Experimental group.
2. To find out the significant difference between the Post – Test Scores of the Control and Experimental group.
3. To find out the significant difference between Control and Experimental group at the Pre – Test and Post – Test Scores.
4. To find out the effect of Educational Software on Achievement in Chemistry with respect to different variables such as of Gender, Caste and Science Marks secured in Standard X.

Hypotheses

The following hypotheses were formulated to realize the above objectives.

1. There is no significant difference between the Pre- Test and Post – Test Scores of the Control group and Experimental group.
2. There is no significant difference between the Control group and Experimental group at the Pre – Test and Post – Test Scores.
3. There is no influence of Gender, Caste and Science Marks secured in Standard X (SMSX) over the effect of Educational Software on Achievement in Chemistry.

Nature of the Research

The present investigation is Experimental in nature, because the investigators aimed to compare the Effectiveness of Teaching Chemistry to the XI Standard Students through Teaching and through Eureka Educational Software.

Sample Selection

The investigators selected XI Standard Students of Periyar Centenary Memorial Matriculation Higher Secondary School, K.K. Nagar Trichy to carry out the Experiment because the School has been posed with well equipped computer facilities. Based on the half – yearly performance of the Students, they are divided into two groups. The total number of students 79, of which 37 belonged to Control Group and 42 belonged to Experimental Group.

Development of Tool

The Eureka Educational Software, 'Designmate' was the Dependent Variable and the Achievement in Chemistry was the Independent Variable. The Eureka Educational Software was given to the Post Graduate Teachers who are handling Chemistry in the nearby schools for content validity. The opinion of them was highly satisfactory.

The developed Achievement test questionnaires were framed by the investigators with the guidance of the subject experts covering the following items such as Knowledge, Understanding, Application and Skill. These questionnaires were validated by Test – Retest method among the Student of XI Standard. The obtained 'r' value 0.74 shows that the tool is highly valuable. Thus the Validity and Reliability of the tool were established. The developed Achievement Test in Chemistry was conducted before and after the treatment for both Control and Experiment Groups. Then the Investigators taught Chemistry through Educational Software to the Experimental Group. Similar topics in Chemistry were taught through Lecture Method to the Control Group.

After the finalization of the tool, the investigators had given 40 items to the Students. Each item was in the form of multiple choices with an incomplete statement. For each item four alternative answers were given. Only one was the correct answer. The Students were requested to write the response in the form of correct alpha bate a, b, c and d. Each × responses carry 1 mark.

Data Analysis

Thus the data collected in this manner undertake analysis by using different statistical technique. Mean and SD were calculated for each Variables to calculate 't' values which is the test of significance of the difference between two means. The following tables contained the data regarding the Control group and Experimental group with the following variables such as Gender, Caste and SMSX.

Table 1: Mean and SD of the Student towards Achievement Score for different Category of Control Group

Sl.No	Variable	Category	Sample Size	Mean		SD	
				Pre-Test	Post-Test	Pre-Test	Post-Test
01.	Gender	Boys	18	20.83	65.97	9.09	13.31
		Girls	19	15.53	62.5	12.05	17.37
02.	Caste	OC/BC	23	22.07	65.43	11.48	16.57
		MBC/SC/ST	14	11.61	62.14	6.09	13.69
03.	SMSX	Above 70%	21	21.55	68.21	10.73	11.34
		Below 70%	16	13.59	62.66	9.72	16.31
04.	Total		37	18.11	64.19	11.03	15.63

From the above table 1it is revealed that the average Mean Score of the Student towards Achievement Score for different category is 18.11 at Pre-Test level and 64.19 at Post-Test level which show the effectiveness of Lecture Method. Moreover at the Pre-Test level the minimum score at the is 11.61 and the maximum score is 22.07. At the Post-Test level 62.14 is the minimum score and 68.21 is the maximum score.

Table 2: Mean and SD of the Student towards Achievement Score for different Category of Experimental Group

S.No	Variable	Category	Sample Size	Mean		SD	
				Pre-Test	Post-Test	Pre-Test	Post-Test
01.	Gender	Boys	21	25.6	81.67	9.66	10.24
		Girls	21	13.81	70.12	7.82	10.62
02.	Caste	OC/BC	26	21.63	76.44	10.56	11.99
		MBC/SC/ST	16	16.56	74.68	9.84	12.58
03.	SMSX	Above 70%	18	18.89	78.89	10.28	9.33
		Below70%	24	19.9	73.65	11.24	13.11
04.	Total		42	19.70	75.89	15.63	11.93

Above table shows that the average Mean Score of the Student towards Achievement Score for different category is 19.70 at Pre-Test level and 75.89 at Post-Test level which show the Eureka Educational Software has considerable effect in Teaching Chemistry. Moreover at the Pre- Test level the minimum score is 13.81 and the maximum score is 25.6. At the Post-Test level 70.12 is the minimum score and 81.67 is the maximum score.

Table 3: Significant Difference between the Mean scores of Control Group and Experimental Group at Pre – Test level

Group	N	Mean	SD	t value	Remarks
Control	37	18.11	11.03	0.661	NS
Experimental	42	19.70	10.58		

NS: Not significant

The above table 3 reveals that the obtained mean Student Achievement Scores in Chemistry of the Control group and Experimental group are more or less same. The calculated 't' value also indicates there is no significant difference at 5% level between Control group and Experimental group at Pre- Test level. Hence the stated Null Hypothesis is that, there is no significant difference between the mean Student Achievement Scores in Chemistry of the Control group and Experimental group at the Pre – Test level is accepted.

Table 4: Significant Difference between the Mean scores of Control Group and Experimental Group at Post – Test level

Group	N	Mean	SD	t value	Remarks
Control	37	64.19	15.63	**4.01**	S
Experimental	42	75.89	11.93		

S: Significant

It is evident from the table 4 that the obtained mean value of Experimental group is greater than the control group. The calculated 't' value shows that there is significant difference between the Control group and Experimental group. Hence the stated Null hypothesis that there is no significant difference between Student Achievement Scores in Chemistry of Control group and Experimental group at Post -Test level is rejected.

Table 5: Influence of various Category over the performance of the Control Group and Experimental Group at Pre – Test level

Category	Group	N	Mean	SD	t value	Remarks
Boys	Control	18	20.83	9.09	1.59	NS
	Experimental	21	25.6	9.66		
Girls	Control	19	15.53	12.05	0.54	NS
	Experimental	21	13.81	7.82		
OC/BC	Control	23	22.07	11.48	0.14	NS
	Experimental	26	21.63	10.56		
MBC/SC/ST	Control	14	11.61	6.09	1.68	NS
	Experimental	16	16.56	9.84		
Above 70%	Control	21	21.55	10.73	0.78	NS
	Experimental	18	18.89	10.28		
Below 70%	Control	16	13.59	9.72	1.88	NS
	Experimental	24	19.9	11.24		

The above table 5 shows that the calculated 't' values of Control group and Experimental group at the Pre-Test level at various Categories has no significant difference at 5 % level. Hence it is concluded that Gender, Caste, SMSX has no influence over the performance of Control group and Experimental group at the Pre-Test level. Therefore the stated Null hypothesis is that, there is no influence of Gender, Caste, SMSX over the performance of Student Achievement Scores in Chemistry of the Control group and Experimental group at the Pre-Test is accepted.

Table 6: Significant Difference between the Mean scores of Pre-Test and Post-Test for Control Group

Test	N	Mean	SD	t value	Remarks
Pre	37	18.11	11.03	**14.62**	S
Post	37	64.19	15.63		

It is evident from the table 6 that the obtained mean value of Post-Test is greater than the Pre-Test. The calculated't' value shows that there is significant difference between the Pre-Test and Post-Test conducted for the Control group. Hence the stated Null hypothesis that there is no significant difference between Student Achievement Scores in Chemistry for the Pre-Test and Post-Test of Control group is rejected.

Table 7: Significant Difference between the Mean scores of Pre-Test and Post-Test for Experimental Group

Test	N	Mean	SD	t value	Remarks
Pre	42	19.70	10.58	**22.61**	S
Post	42	75.89	11.93		

The above table 7 reveals that the obtained mean Student Achievement Scores in Chemistry of the Post-Test is greater than Pre-Test of Experimental group. The calculated 't' value also indicates there is significant difference at 5% level between Pre-Test and Post-Test of Experimental group. Hence the stated Null Hypothesis is that, there is no significant difference between the mean Student Achievement Scores in Chemistry for the Pre-Test and Post-Test of Experimental group is rejected.

Table 8: Influence of Gender over the performance of the Control Group and Experimental Group at Post – Test level

Gender	Group	N	Mean	SD	t value	Remarks
Boys	Control	18	65.97	13.31	**4.02**	S
	Experimental	21	81.67	10.24		
Girls	Control	19	62.5	17.37	1.52	NS
	Experimental	21	70.12	10.62		

The above table 8 shows that the calculated 't' values of Control group and Experimental group at the Post- Test level of the Boys has significant difference between the mean scores at 5 % level. The above table also reveals that the calculated 't' values of Control group and Experimental group at the Post-Test level of the Girls has no significant difference between the mean scores at 5 % level. Therefore the stated Null hypothesis is that, except Boys the Girls has no influence over the performance of Student Achievement Scores in Chemistry of the Control group and Experimental group at the Post- Test is accepted.

Table 9: Influence of Caste over the performance of the Control Group and Experimental Group at Post-Test level

Caste	Group	N	Mean	SD	t value	Remarks
OC/BC	Control	23	65.43	16.57	**2.63**	S
	Experimental	26	76.44	11.99		
MBC/SC/ST	Control	14	62.14	13.69	**2.62**	S
	Experimental	16	74.68	12.58		

The calculated 't' values from the above table reveals that Control group and Experimental group at the Post -Test level of the Caste has significant difference between the mean scores at 5 % level. The mean values of the above table shows that there is influence of caste over the performance of Control group and Experimental group at the Post- Test level. Hence the stated Null Hypothesis is that, there is influence of caste over the performance of Student Achievement Scores in Chemistry of the Control group and Experimental group at the Post-Test is rejected.

Table 10: Influence of Students secured Science Marks in Standard X over the performance of the Control Group and Experimental Group at Post-Test level

SMSX	Group	N	Mean	SD	t value	Remarks
Above 70%	Control	21	68.21	11.34	**3.43**	S
	Experimental	18	78.89	9.33		
Below 70%	Control	16	62.66	16.31	**2.45**	S
	Experimental	24	73.65	13.11		

It is evident from the table 10 that the obtained mean value of Experimental group is greater than the Control group. The calculated 't' value shows that there is significant difference between the Control group and Experimental group at the Post-Test level with respect to SMSX at 5 % level. The mean values of the above table shows that there is influence of SMSX over the performance of Control group and Experimental group at the Post-Test level. Hence the stated Null Hypothesis is that, there is influence of SMSX over the performance of Student Achievement Scores in Chemistry of the Control group and Experimental group at the Post-Test is rejected.

Findings & Discussion

The salient findings of the study are i) the Eureka Educational Software has considerable effect in Teaching Chemistry, ii) there is a significant difference between the mean scores of Pre- Test and Post-Test level for both Control Group and Experimental Group, iii) Gender, Caste and SMSX has no influence over the performance of Student Achievement Scores in Chemistry of the Control group and Experimental group at the Pre-Test level, iii) Caste and SMSX has influence over the performance of Student Achievement Scores in Chemistry of the Control group and Experimental group at the Post-Test level and v) Experimental group Boys show significant higher mean scores in the Achievement Scores than the Control group, but Girls has no influence over the performance of Student Achievement Scores in Chemistry of the Control group and Experimental group.

While conducting the Pre-Test it was observed that both Control and Experimental groups posses similar level of pervious knowledge on the selected contents in Chemistry. The same trend was observed with respect to different variables such as Gender, Caste and SMSX. When the analysis was made between Pre-Test and Post-Test Scores of the Control and Experimental groups it was observed that both methods of teaching such as traditional Lecture Method and Educational Software method, Educational Software method is found to be effective method. While comparing the Mean Achievement Scores between Control and Experimental group it was observed that students who learnt through Eureka Educational Software score significant higher than the Control group Students. The significant difference of the Experimental group may be due to the reason that the Eureka Educational Software has incorporated with interactive presentation, animated movies, special effects and puzzles, these special features might have attracted the Experimental Students to score more marks.

It is interesting to note when comparing the Achievements of Girls Students between Control and Experiment groups the effectiveness was not significant as the Girls Students might not show interest towards Computer Assisted Instruction at XI Standard level.

Education Implications

This Experimental Study established the positive result on Achievement, so the Educational Institutions may be encouraged to use the Computer Assisted Instruction for the Teaching Learning process. Subject experts may concentrate on preparing Software packages in all the units of the all the subjects and distribute them to Schools. This may make the Students more interest towards Educations and it also make the Teachers to save their time.

Conclusions

Eureka Educational Software is more suitable method for teaching Chemistry at XI Standard level. Eureka Educational Software is the one of the best method in the Teaching Learning process of Chemistry for XI Standard Students without considering the individual variables such as Gender, Caste and SMSX this is due to the subject contents are taught through more animations and interactions. Due to this Educational Software Students concentrations increased and they easily understood the subject contents. At the Post- Test level the Girls shows no significant difference in the Achievement Scores in Chemistry of the Control group and Experimental group.

Reference

1. Ramesh Chandra (2004). Impact of Media and Technology in Education, Kalpaz Publications, New Delhi.
2. Rao, V.K.(2005). Instructional Technolgy, APH Publishing Corporation, New Delhi.
3. Rawat, S.C. (2004). Essentials of Educational Technology, R.Lall Book Depot, Meerut.
4. Zaidi, S.M.(2004). Educational Technology, Anmol Publisher Pvt. Ltd New Delhi.

❐

19.

Educational-Digital Skill

INTRODUCTION

There is a tremendous revolution in science and technology. Information in communication technologies have a deep cultural revolution changing. There is a need to make a realistic assessment of what technology cannot do to reach a plateau of productivity when the technology consistently delivers to realistic goals.

The impact of science and technology among students

Digital skill is a vast technique used by all people. Educational technology and mobile learning, multi- media learning are all digital skill. Science is a boon. Man has discovered many wonderful things from the treasure of developing every day. It has made our life easier, happier and more secure. Science and technology has conquered time and space. It has made very good communication and made the transport easier. With the help of science and technology, modern medicine and medical treatments, the doctors save the life of sick people from the jaws of death. Many organs are now transplanted. It is used in the field of agriculture. The impact of science and technology among students in the field is both good and bad.

Science laboratory, space centre ISRO are taken in the highest form. Television, telecommunication, type- recorder, films, LCD projectors, digital and white board, e- learning, e-teaching, teleconferencing, teaching machine cell phones such as all types of multimedia are boons to us. But the students are affected by this because of misusing. So they blamed science. We cannot blame science. It is a wonderful boon.

Digital skill in website

By the wrong use of face book, web site, web-camera, especially cell phones, net connection, lab top etc. Science and technology become down. But once for all where we use science and technology in proper, correct and perfect way it is a boon to us otherwise it is curse and demon to us.

A secondary Information and Communication Technology curriculum should contribute to the building up of teams of professionals with these new competencies. The use of Information and Communication Technology cuts across all aspects of economic and social life. Technological developments in Information and Communication Technology are very rapid. Technology quickly becomes obsolete requiring new skills and knowledge to be mastered frequently. Adaptation is only possible when based on a sound understanding of the principles and concepts of Information and Communication Technology.

REVIEW OF LITERATURE

Lei, Jing (2010) studied on Quantity versus Quality: A New Approach to Examine the Relationship between Technology Use and Student Outcomes. It is found that that to examine the relationship between technology use and student outcomes, the quality of technology use--how, and what, technology is used--is a more significant factor than the quantity of technology use--how much technology is used. This argument was exemplified by an empirical study that used both angles to examine the association between technology use and student outcomes. When only the quantity of technology use was examined, no significant association was observed. However, when the quality of technology was examined by investigating the specific types of technology uses, a significant association was identified between technology use and all student outcomes. Furthermore, different types of technology use showed different influences on specific student outcomes. General technology uses were positively associated with student technology proficiency, while subject-specific technology uses were negatively associated with student technology proficiency. Social-communication technology uses were significantly positively associated with developmental outcomes such as self-esteem and positive attitude towards school. Entertainment/exploration technology use showed significant positive association with student learning habits. None of these technology uses had significant influence on student academic outcome.

Chen, Rong-Ji (2010) studied on Investigating Models for Preservice Teachers' Use of Technology to Support Student-Centered Learning. The study addressed two limitations of previous research on factors related to teachers' integration of technology in their teaching. It attempted to test a structural equation model (SEM) of the relationships among a set of variables influencing preservice teachers' use of technology specifically to support student-centered learning. A review of literature led to a path model that provided the design and analysis for the study, which involved 206 preservice teachers in the United States. The results show that the proposed model had a moderate fit to the observed data, and a more parsimonious model was found to have a better fit. In addition, preservice teachers' self-efficacy of teaching with technology had the strongest influence on technology use, which was mediated by their perceived value of teaching and learning with technology. School's contextual factors had moderate influence on technology use. Moreover, the effect of preservice teachers' training on student-centered technology use was mediated by both perceived value and self-efficacy of technology. The implications for teacher preparation include close collaboration between teacher education program and field experience, focusing on specific technology uses.

Eisenberg, Mike; Johnson, Doug; Berkowitz, Bob (2010) studied on Information, Communications, and Technology (ICT) Skills Curriculum Based on the Big6 Skills Approach to Information Problem-Solving. There is clear and widespread agreement among the public and educators that all students need to be proficient technology users. Technology literacy is among the attributes that appear in nearly every set of "21st Century Skills." However, while districts spend a great deal of money on technology, there seems to be only a vague notion of what technology literacy really means. Defining and describing technology skills is only a first step to assure all children become proficient information and technology users. Other critical elements will include a teacher-supported scope and sequence of skills, well designed projects, and effective assessments. Equally essential is fruitful collaboration among classroom teachers, teacher librarians, and technology teachers in order to present students with a unified and integrated approach to ensure that all children master the skills they will need to thrive in an information-rich future. This article presents the "Information, Communications, and Technology (ICT) Skills for Information Problem Solving" curriculum which defines technology capabilities and identifies associated skills based on the Big6 Skills Approach. The Curriculum describes levels of technology proficiency, and in so doing, promotes the skills and concepts basic to information and technology. In an information society, it is essential that students are technologically productive and able to solve information problems effectively and efficiently. This curriculum requires more than teaching computer skills, technology hardware, and software programs in an isolated approach. An effective technology curriculum must be integrated across content areas and grade levels to improve the learning process. Technology is successfully integrated when it seamlessly supports curricular goals. Students learn and refine their technology skills when they work on projects that require them to solve problems and make decisions.

Savage, Robert S.; Erten, Ozlem; Abrami, Philip; Hipps, Geoffrey; Comaskey, Erin; van Lierop, Dea (2010) studied on ABRACADABRA in the Hands of Teachers: The Effectiveness of a Web-Based Literacy Intervention in Grade 1 Language Arts Programs . Each teacher chose to use the program in qualitatively distinct ways that corresponded to the first three stages of Sandholtz, Ringstaff, and Dwyer's (1997) technology integration model, namely: "Entry," "Adoption" and "Adaptation." Growth in literacy between pre- and post-test revealed significant differences associated with technology integration style across all measures of literacy and related language skills. The largest and most-widespread effects were evident for the "Adaptation" group that linked technology content to wider learning themes in the classroom. In terms of overall growth in standardised literacy scores across all six such measures used, Adaptation proved to be 60% more effective than Adoption. Results suggest that explorations of exactly how teachers use technology have important implications for practice as well as for the interpretation of field-based studies of the effectiveness of educational technology.

Jun, Han; Zhuzhu, Wang (2010) studied on Capability Building in Educational Technology for Teachers in China. This paper gives a brief introduction to the project called Education Technology Capacity Building Plan for All Primary and Secondary Teachers now being implemented in China. Because information and communication technology skills training cannot match the demand of teachers' professional development, the Chinese Ministry of Education established the education technology standard for teachers and launched the project. This paper introduced the features of standard training and testing, and discusses the output and influence of the project.

McGarr, Oliver (2010) studied on Education for Sustainable Development in Technology Education in Irish Schools: A Curriculum Analysis. This paper explores the integration of Education for Sustainable Development (ESD) in technology education and the extent to which it is currently addressed in curriculum documents and state examinations in technology education at post-primary level in Ireland. This analysis is conducted amidst the backdrop of considerable change in technology education at post-primary level. The analysis of the provision of technology education found, that among the range of technology related subjects offered, the study of Technology and Society is only addressed in one in a comprehensive manner. The paper discusses the implications of this limited integration, examines the factors inhibiting greater integration of ESD and outlines opportunities for future development.

Waring, Scott M. (2010) studied on The Impact of a Technology Coordinator's Belief System upon Using Technology to Create a Community's History. As it has been shown that teachers of social studies content are less likely than teachers of other content areas to utilize technology in their classroom, this study focuses on one instructional technology coordinators' beliefs towards technology, instruction, and students and how these beliefs impacted how technology was utilized during a technology-enriched community history project with a group of fourth-grade students. It was determined that the instructional technology coordinators' beliefs included the following: (a) technology should serve as a tool and should be seamlessly integrated into the curriculum; (b) the teacher should construct meaningful experiences that allow students to become engaged in the learning process; however, before guiding student discovery, the teacher needs to explicitly teach basic technological skills; (c) and all students are able to learn and are capable of engaging in independent problem solving and critical thinking at some level. Her beliefs manifested themselves daily, particularly in the way that she approached instruction and integrated technology seamlessly into the curriculum.

Through this study, it was found that the technology coordinator's beliefs toward technology, instruction, and her students directly impacted how technology was used in her classroom.

Jun, Han; Zhuzhu, Wang (2010) studied on Capability Building in Educational Technology for Teachers in China. This paper gives a brief introduction to the project called Education Technology Capacity Building Plan for All Primary and Secondary Teachers now being implemented in China. Because information and communication technology skills training cannot match the demand of teachers' professional development, the Chinese Ministry of Education established the education technology standard for teachers and launched the project. This paper introduced the features of standard training and testing, and discusses the output and influence of the project.

Ruzic-Dimitrijevic, Ljiljana; Dimitrijevic, Maja (2010) studied on Challenges IT Instructors Face in the Self-Education Process. We find that the earlier the instructors graduated, the smaller is the chance they studied the technologies similar to the ones they teach. We found that none of the surveyed instructors who graduated before 1979 teach a technology they studied. The analysis of the survey also supports the second hypothesis. The results show that 70% of the IT instructors have to change the course syllabus every 2-3 years due to the technology changes. We also found that the majority of the instructors primarily use textbooks and online tutorials to self teach new technologies, which supports the third hypothesis. By comparison, they take courses given by others and work on real life projects far less often. In contrast, most instructors agree that taking courses and working on projects would greatly help them in their self-education. Most instructors (16 out of 20) assert that the lack of time stops them from doing so, which according to the survey is found to be one of the major challenges they face in the process of self-education, supporting the fourth hypothesis. Considering the results of our research, as well as our own experience, we have identified a list of activities that make the process of self-education more efficient and/or effective for IT instructors. These activities include taking on-line tutorials, creating software programs using the environment/ language/tools covered in the courses, working on real life projects, taking organized courses, attending IT/CS conferences, seminars, and workshops, collecting experience from industry people, and using the help of advanced students. However, in order to create the time for IT instructors to apply the self-learning methods and stay on top of the new technologies, we conclude that it may be necessary that the university policy include the time for self-learning as a significant part of IT instructors' everyday duties, i.e., as a part of their "job description".

Larson, Lotta; Kuhn, Cyndi Danner; Collins, Royce Ann; Balthazor, Gerri; Ribble, Mike; Miller, Teresa Northern (2009) studied on Technology Instruction: Fixing the Disconnect. High school students spend much of their educational journeys immersed in "old" literacies of paper, pencil, and print books. But outside of the classroom, they are exposed to information and communication technologies--such as blogs, wikis, Internet browsers, multimedia, social networking sites, and a wide range of software--each of which demand new literacies. This disconnect is a serious problem for schools because it reflects a decline in school's relevancy to students' futures, and the gap between how schools teach and how students learn will only grow over time. The first step in updating a school's technology and instruction is to revisit and revise current vision statements by facilitating conversations with all stakeholders about expectations for student skills upon graduation. Vision setting must include the new literacies. Teachers and education leaders must model expectations and support visionary teaching and learning through technology. To make that happen, they need instructional technology specialists who not only have a strong knowledge of hardware, networks, and equipment maintenance but also understand the art of teaching and how to enhance and enrich the daily curriculum by integrating technology. To do this, instructional technology staff members and those creating the curriculum must engage in ongoing dialogue to ensure that computer language is translated into the language of teaching and is directly related to what teachers want to do in their classrooms. For schools to successfully integrate technology, leaders must encourage and support strong relationships between teachers and technology support staff members. Schools must also provide easy access to technology in classrooms so that teachers can effectively integrate technology into the curriculum. Limited resources and complicated check-out procedures often contribute to lack of use. In addition, frustrations over blocked sites or limited access to online resources prevent teachers from integrating technology. Leaders, teachers, and technology staff members need ongoing communication with one another to share needs, frustrations, and solutions. Schools must move ahead quickly. It may be understandable for teachers and leaders to be a bit behind in the use of technology, but it is no longer adequate or appropriate to hold students back. Students today will be leaders in a global society, and technology can connect them to that world in ways that were unimaginable 10 years ago. School leaders need to join students in their world--which includes all of the new literacies--so that everyone can function and contribute to the future.

OBJECTIVES

1. To study the level of teachers attitude towards using new technology in teaching
2. To find out whether there is any significant relationship between teachers attitude towards the use of new technology and their interest in teaching.

METHODOLOGY

The methodology adopted for the study is explained in detail. The sampling technique, size of the sample, variables of the study, description of the tool used and administration of tool are elaborated.

Sample

The study was conducted on 100 school teachers, Coimbatore district, Tamil Nadu.

Data Collection

Primary data, required for the present research work were collected by conducting direct interviews using questionnaire. All the respondents were given sufficient information about the study. These respondents were provided with the same questionnaires. They were also informed that they have to answer in the same fashion.

ANALYSIS AND INTERPRETATION

Gender and attitude towards the use of new technology

Null Hypothesis 1

There is no significant difference between male and female teachers attitude towards the use of new technology.

Table 1: The Significance of the difference ('t' value) between mean scores of male and female teacher's attitude towards the use of new technology

Gender	N	Mean	SD	't' value	Level of Significance (0.05)
Male	50	100.30	11.81	4.89	Significant
Female	50	107.30	12.57		

It is evident from the table the calculated 't' value is 4.89 is significant at 0.05 level. Hence, the framed null hypothesis is rejected and research hypothesis is accepted. It is inferred that there is significant difference found between male and female teachers attitude towards the use of new technology.

Qualification and attitude towards the use of new technology

Null Hypothesis 2

There is no significant difference between undergraduate and post graduate teachers with respect to their attitude towards the use of new technology.

Table 2: The significance of the difference ('t' value) between undergraduate and post graduate teachers with respect to their attitude towards the use of new technology.

Qualification	N	Mean	SD	't' value	Level of Significance (0.05)
Under graduate	35	103.64	11.44	0.28	Not Significant
Post graduate	65	103.23	13.53		

It is evident from the table the calculated 't' value is 0.28 which is not significant at 0.05 level. Hence, the framed null hypothesis is accepted. It shows that there is no significant difference between undergraduate and post graduate teachers with respect to their attitude towards the use of new technology.

Locality of the School and attitude towards the use of new technology

Null Hypothesis 3

There is no significant difference between rural and urban school teachers attitude towards the use of new technology.

Table 3: The Significance of the difference ('t' value) between rural and urban school teachers attitude towards the use of new technology

Locality of the school	N	Mean	SD	't' value	Level of Significance (0.05)
Rural	65	103.42	11.23	0.06	Not Significant
Urban	35	103.33	14.15		

It is evident from the table the calculated 't' value is 0.06 which is not significant at 0.05 level. Hence, the framed null hypothesis is accepted. It shows that there is no significant difference between rural and urban school teachers attitude towards the use of new technology.

Type of School and attitude towards the use of new technology

Null Hypothesis 4

There is no significant difference between private and government school teachers attitude towards the use of new technology.

Table 4: The Significance of the difference ('t' value) between private and government school teachers attitude towards the use of new technology

Type of School	N	Mean	SD	t'' value	Level of Significance (0.05)
Private	65	104.79	11.54	1.26	Not Significant
Government	35	102.78	13.01		

It is evident from the table the calculated 't' value is 1.26 which is not significant at 0.05 level. Hence, the framed null hypothesis is accepted. It shows that there is no significant difference between private and government school teachers attitude towards the use of new technology.

Level of teaching and attitude towards the use of new technology

Null Hypothesis 5

There is no significant difference between secondary and higher secondary school teachers attitude towards the use of new technology.

Table 5: The Significance of the difference ('t' test) between secondary and higher secondary school teachers attitude towards the use of new technology

Level of teaching	N	Mean	SD	't' value	Level of Significance (0.05)
Secondary School	60	102.12	12.12	1.85	Not Significant
Higher secondary School	40	104.82	13.03		

It is evident from the table the calculated 't' value is 1.85 which is not significant at 0.05 level. Hence, the framed null hypothesis is accepted. It is inferred that there is no significant difference between secondary and higher secondary school teachers attitude towards the use of new technology.

Teaching Experience and attitude towards the use of new technology

Null Hypothesis 6

There is no significant difference among teachers who have different years of teaching experience with respect to their attitude towards the use of new technology.

Table 6: The Significance of the difference ('F' test) among school teachers with respect to their attitude towards the use of new technology

Teaching Experience	Sum of Squares	Mean Squares	df	'F' Value	Level of Significance (0.05)
Between Groups	2281.690	1140.845	2	7.48	Significant
Within Groups	45273.227	152.435	97		
Total	47554.917	-	99		

It is evident from the table the calculated 'F' value is 7.48 which is significant at 0.05 level. Hence, the framed null hypothesis is rejected and research hypothesis is accepted. It is inferred that there is significant difference among teachers who have different years of teaching experience with respect to their attitude towards the use of new technology.

Table 7: The Significance of the difference ('t' test) between teachers who have different years of teaching experience with respect to their attitude towards the use of new technology

Teaching experience	N	Mean	SD	't' value	Level of Significance (0.05)
Below 10 years	49	109.33	11.05	3.06	Significant
10-20 years	20	103.03	12.80		
Above 20 years	31	101.67	12.47	4.16	Significant
Below 10 years	49	109.33	11.05		
10-20 years	20	103.03	12.80	0.81	Not Significant
Above 20 years	31	101.67	12.47		

From table, it is revealed that there is significant difference between teachers who have below 10 years of teaching experience and 10-20 years of teaching experience and teachers who have above 20 years of teaching experience and below 10 years of teaching experience. Whereas no significant difference is found between teachers who have above 20 years of teaching experience and 10-20 years of teaching experience.

CORRELATION ANALYSIS

Correlation Analysis between teachers attitude towards the use of new technology and interest in teaching.

One of the important objectives of the present investigation is to study the significant relationship between teacher's attitude towards the use of new technology and interest in teaching. For this purpose, the investigator applied the co-efficient of correlation ('r'). The computed values are given in the table. The investigator also framed a null hypothesis for testing the relationship between teacher's attitude towards the use of new technology and interest in teaching.

Null hypothesis 7

There is no significant relationship between teacher's attitude towards the use of new technology and interest in teaching.

Table 7: Co-efficient of Correlation between teacher's attitude towards the use of new technology and interest in teaching

Correlation	N	'r' value	Level of Significance at 0.05 level
Teacher's attitude towards the use of new technology and interest in teaching	100	0.56	Significant

It is evident from the table the computed correlation coefficient 'r' for entire sample is 0.56, which is significant at 0.05 level. Hence, the framed null hypothesis is rejected. It is inferred that there is significant relationship found between teacher's attitude towards the use of new technology and their interest in teaching.

SUGGESTIONS

The present study gives a clear-cut view about the present position of teachers attitude towards the use of new technology and their interest in teaching. Based on the important findings stated earlier the following recommendations are suggested.

1. Teachers must be provided with adequate opportunities to enhance their knowledge in new technologies and equipments. The government should provide more effective environment through schools for them to improve their skills in application of new technologies in teaching.
2. Periodical in-service training programmes should be organized to keep their interest and quest in teaching.
3. The finding of the present study reveals that the teachers have neutral attitude towards the use of new technology in teaching and low interest in teaching. This indicates that the Heads of the institutions must look into the varied problems that influence the interest of teachers and find amicable solutions to their difficulties.
4. More activities should be planned in the curriculum to bring forth different modes of creative expressions which will provide competition and generate interest of teachers in teaching.
5. Sincere work and involved performances of teachers must be recognized and honoured by the authorities. And application of innovative methods and technologies in instruction must be encouraged.
6. In addition with the above recommendation the government and all the other concerned authorities should realize the problems of experienced teachers and provide conductive environment of growth and mutual help of teachers should be ensured.

CONCLUSION

The present study is conducted on teachers attitude towards the use of new technologies in teaching and their interest in teaching. The findings of the present study revealed that the teachers have neutral attitude towards the use of new technology and low interest in teaching. Therefore, the authorities and government should find suitable measures to improve the interest of teachers in teaching and the application of innovative technologies in Teaching Learning Process.

REFERENCES

1. Larson, Lotta; Kuhn, Cyndi Danner; Collins, Royce Ann; Balthazor, Gerri; Ribble, Mike; Miller, Teresa Northern (2009) Technology Instruction: Fixing the Disconnect. Principal Leadership, v10 n4 p54-58.

2. Chen, Rong-Ji (2010) Investigating Models for Preservice Teachers' Use of Technology to Support Student-Centered Learning. Computers & Education, v55 n1 p32-42.
3. Eisenberg, Mike; Johnson, Doug; Berkowitz, Bob (2010) Information, Communications, and Technology (ICT) Skills Curriculum Based on the Big6 Skills Approach to Information Problem-Solving. Library Media Connection, v28 n6 p24-27.
4. Jun, Han; Zhuzhu, Wang(2010) Capability Building in Educational Technology for Teachers in China British Journal of Educational Technology, v41 n4 p607-611.
5. Lei, Jing (2010) Quantity versus Quality: A New Approach to Examine the Relationship between Technology Use and Student Outcomes. 2010.
6. Lesisko, Lee J.; Wright, Robert J.; O'Hern, Brenda (2010) Technology Integration: A Best Practice Perspective. Online Submission, Paper presented at the Annual Meeting of the Eastern Educational Research Association (Savannah, GA, Feb 10-13, 2010).
7. McGarr, Oliver (2010) Education for Sustainable Development in Technology Education in Irish Schools: A Curriculum Analysis. International Journal of Technology and Design Education, v20 n3 p317-332.
8. Ruzic-Dimitrijevic, Ljiljana; Dimitrijevic, Maja (2010) Challenges IT Instructors Face in the Self-Education Process. Journal of Information Technology Education, v9 pIIP-35-IIP-48.
9. Savage, Robert S.; Erten, Ozlem; Abrami, Philip; Hipps, Geoffrey; Comaskey, Erin; van Lierop, Dea (2010) ABRACADABRA in the Hands of Teachers: The Effectiveness of a Web-Based Literacy Intervention in Grade 1 Language Arts Programs . Computers & Education, v55 n2 p911-922.
10. Shapley, Kelly; Sheehan, Daniel; Maloney, Catherine; Caranikas-Walker, Fanny (2010) Effects of Technology Immersion on Teachers' Growth in Technology Competency, Ideology, and Practices. Journal of Educational Computing Research, v42 n1 p1-33.

❐

20.

Effectiveness of Blended Learning Programme in Teaching Biology at Higher Secondary School Students

INTRODUCTION

The recent research in science education has focused on instruction that is specific science content, specific instructional strategies and how they are related to biology learning contexts and instructional outcomes. In the present scientific and technological age, the conventional teaching methods are not sufficient to arouse interest among the students and do not meet up to the intellectual, psychological and emotional needs of the students in the new millennium. The methods of teaching biology need to be changed.

In a vast country like India, enormous work is now being done in the field of education but it is still not possible to equip each and every higher and higher secondary school with all the facilities for teaching biology in the near future. Most of the higher secondary schools, both in rural and urban area are suffering from lack of modern science laboratories. They need equally advanced gadgets to support their education. Technology enables students get a live vision of life's aspects and scientific factors. Any diagram can be explained in detail with 3d effect, it helps the student to understand the lesson clearly. Keeping in mind the investigator felt it appropriate to use blended learning for the teaching of the concepts in biology topics included in the XI standard biology syllabus (Tamil Medium).

BLENDED LEARNING

Blended learning provides platform to attract the senses of the learner for easy and happy learning. Blended learning is a programme which integrates teaching learning process with different leaning environment. Its rapid growth facilitated by the internet and other emerging technology cloud computing and social networking.

"Blended learning is the thoughtful fusion of face-to-face and online learning experiences. The basic principle is that face-to-face oral communication and online written communication are optimally integrated such that the strengths of each are blended into a unique learning experience congruent with the context and intended educational purpose."

Blended learning – an instructional practice that combines teaching methods from both face-to-face instruction and online learning, gives to educational institutions new approaches and strategies for addressing the challenges they face and for taking advantage of the exciting new learning opportunities that are now available.

Blended learning does not exclude the traditional learning methods, but adds new and modern methods as: IT tools (email, web, chat, online conferences, e-learning platforms), workshops, individual project groups, practical demonstrations, etc.

OBJECTIVES OF THE STUDY

The objectives of the study as follows

1. To find out the effectiveness of blended learning programme for the teaching of biology at higher secondary level.
2. To compare the effectiveness of blended learning programme in the teaching of biology with conventional method of teaching biology.

HYPOTHESES OF THE STUDY

The following null hypotheses have been formulated

1. There is no significant difference between the experimental group and control group in the achievement of biology at pre test level.
2. There is no significant difference between the experimental group and control group in the achievement of biology at posttest level.
3. There is no significant difference between the pretest and posttest in the achievement of biology for the experimental group.
4. There is no significant difference between the pretest and posttest in the achievement of biology for the control group.

SAMPLE

The sample of the study consists of 100 students studying in XI standard under State Board syllabus at perambalur district. The sample includes both boys and girls.

TOOLS USED

The following tools had been used for the present study:

An achievement test in biology constructed and validated by the investigators

Blended learning programme was developed by the investigator for the teaching of the concepts in biology topics included in the XI standard biology syllabus.

The progrmme was arranged logically based on the psychological principles of learning. Experimental design was adopted. For the experimentation pretest was conducted and sample was divided into two groups. The students of the experimental group were taught with the blended learning progrmme and the control group through the conventional method. After the treatment period the posttest was administered. The collected data were subjected to statistical analysis and the results obtained were interpreted.

TESTING OF HYPOTHESES

Hypothesis 1: There is no significant difference between the experimental group and control group in the achievement of biology at pre test level.

The'
t' test applied to test the significance of difference between the mean achievement test scores of the experimental group and control group of pretest level.

Table 1: Mean Achievement Test Scores of the Experimental Group Compared with that of the Control Group at Pretest level

Groups	N	Mean	S.D	't' value	Level of Significance at 0.05 level
Experimental	30	20.43	2.09	0.46	Not significant
Control	30	19.63	1.87		

The table indicates that the 't' value is not significant at 0.05 level. The students of the experimental group do not differ significantly from the students of the control group in the mean achievement test scores at pre test level.

Hypothesis 2: There is no significant difference between the experimental group and control group in the achievement of biology at posttest level

The 't' test applied to test the significance of difference between the mean achievement test scores of the experimental group and control group of posttest level.

Table 2: Mean Achievement Test Scores of the Experimental Group Compared with that of the Control Group at Posttest level

Groups	N	Mean	S.D	't' value	Level of Significance at 0.01 level
Experimental	30	36.40	3.96	15.08	significant
Control	30	20.10	5.14		

The table indicates that the 't' value is significant at 0.01 level. Hence there is there is a significant difference between the two groups. As indicated by the mean value, it can be concluded that the students of the experimental group fared better in the achievement test than the students of the control group. This shows that learning with the help of blended learning programme will increase the achievement of the students better than learning through the conventional method.

Hypothesis 3: There is no significant difference between the pretest and posttest in the achievement of biology for the experimental group.

The 't' test applied to test the significance of difference between test scores of the pretest with that of the posttest for the experimental group.

Table 3: Mean Achievement Test Scores of Pretest Compared with that of the Posttest for the Experimental Group

Groups	N	Mean	S.D	't' value	Level of Significance at 0.01 level
Experimental	30	20.43	2.07	20.52	Significant
Control	30	37.40	3.96		

Table 3 indicates that the't' value is significant at 0.01 level. Hence, it could be concluded that there is a significant difference between the mean achievement test scores of the pretest and posttest for the experimental group. The higher mean value in the posttest shows that the students fared better in the posttest than in the pretest. This shows that the blended learning programme has helped the students to score more in the posttest.

Hypothesis 4: There is no significant difference between the pretest and posttest in the achievement of biology for the control group.

The 't' test applied to test the significance of difference between the mean achievement test scores of the pretest with that of the posttest for the control group.

Table 4: Mean Achievement Test Scores of Pretest Compared with that of the Posttest for the Control Group

Groups	N	Mean	S.D	't' value	Level of Significance at 0.05 level
Experimental	30	19.76	1.87	0.034	Not significant
Control	30	20.00	5.06		

Table 4 indicates that the 't' value is not significant at 0.05 level. Hence, it could be concluded that there is no significant difference between the mean achievement test scores of the pretest and posttest for the control group.

FINDINGS OF THE STUDY

1. There is no significant difference between the experimental group and control group in the achievement of biology at pretest level.
2. There is a significant difference between the experimental group and control group in the achievement of biology at posttest level. The students leaning with the help of blended learning programme fared better in biology than in students learning through the conventional method.
3. There is a significant difference between the mean achievement test scores of the pretest and posttest for the experimental group. This shows that the blended learning programme has helped the students to score more marks in the posttest.
4. There is a significant difference between the mean achievement test scores of the pretest and posttest for the control group. This shows that the conventional method of teaching will not help the students to score more marks in the posttest.

CONCLUSION

In the field of education is not possible to equip the teaching leaning in higher and higher secondary level because most of the higher secondary schools suffering from lack of modern methods of teaching, they still follow the conventional method of teaching in higher secondary level. This should be change in the modern era; they should follow the blended learning methods in their teaching learning methods because it supports the education department well in advance.

REFERENCE

1. Barbour Michael, et al, (2012), *Online and Blended Learning: A Survey of Policy and Practice of K-12 Schools Around the World*, available at http://www.inacol.org/cms/wpcontent/uploads/2012/11/iNACOL_IntnlReport2011.pdf
2. The Oxford Group (2013), *Blended Learning—Current Use, Challenges and Best Practices*, report 2013, available at http://www.kineo.com/m/0/blended-learning-report-202013.pdf (accessed July 2013)

❐

21.

Awareness on Digital Techniques Applying in Classroom Teaching for Present Generation among Teacher Educators

INTRODUCTION

Modernization is generally regarded as a process of change of traditional society into a society based on technology. As Teaching has entered the Digital age over the last several years, Technology in the Classroom is an area that all Teachers and Students are Embracing. For Teachers who have taught many years before this can be a challenging one. There are many Computer lesson plans, CDs, DVDs, audio e -books and videos available that will help in the transition. Digital Technology in the Classroom involves a lot of time and focus in its infancy, but with the Computer Lesson plans mentioned, it will develop into a fun and creative learning experience for Students and new and exciting challenges for Teachers. The incorporation of Digital technology in the education sector is important to meet the challenges presented by new trends, especially with the Global Communication of Knowledge. It is essential that the Students become familiar with the concept and use of Computer Technology in order to equip them for future job market. Similarly, the teacher can achieve better quality in Teaching Methodology.

Rationale of the Study

Computer plays key role in Education. Learning through Computer is an interesting affair. Now–a-days Digital Technology in Education has become the essential part of the system. In fact Teacher must well aware of the potentiality of the Digital Technology. Government is very much interested in introducing

Computer Technology in Class Room instruction in Teacher Education. Hence the Investigator was interested to know the level of Awareness on Digital techniques applying in classroom teaching for present generation among Teacher Educators.

Statement of the Problem

The important key words used in this problem were:

1. **Awareness:** Alertness, New Idea.
2. **Digital Technology**: The Technology which is used to change the method of Class Room Teaching with the help of Electronic machines and Computer,
3. **Teacher Educators:** Teachers who are working in the Colleges of Education.

Overview of the Study Already Done

Askin Asan(2003) studied on "Computer Technology Awareness by Elementary School Teachers: A Case Study from Turkey" and found that many Teachers were not computer users. At the same time Wheatley, (2003) also studied on increasing computer use in early childhood Teacher Education. The study was found that Teachers lacked a functional Computer Literacy Foundation to new Technology and skills. Nickish and Reinhard (1992) in their study "Teacher Anxiety toward Computer Technology" found that Urban Teachers are used Computer often than Rural Teachers. Sengamalam @ Vanathi (2013) Studied on Awareness on e learning among M.Ed scholars under Bharathidasan University, found that the awareness of scholars whose major subject is Science was found to be superior to the scholars with Arts as major subject.

Objectives of the Study

The objectives of the study were i) To measure the level of Awareness on Digital Technology among Teacher Educators. ii) To measure the level of significant difference on the Awareness on Digital Technology among Male and Female, Rural and Urban, Science and Arts group Teacher Educators.

Method and Materials

It is the Normative Survey method. Investigator constructed a Tool Awareness on Digital Techniques applying in Classroom Teaching for present generation among Teacher Educators. That consists of 40 statements with different dimensions such as Computer in Teaching Learning, Power point Presentation and Internet, which have four point scale such a Strongly Agree, Agree, Disagree and Strongly Disagree. After the Development of the Questionnaire, the Investigator distributed it to Teacher Educators for validation. Their valuable ideas were taken care. Then the questionnaire was given to 10 Teacher Educators by Test - Retest method. The obtained r value 0.84 reveals that the tool is reliable one. Investigators randomly selected 100 Teacher Educators from various Colleges of Education in Perambalur and Trichy Districts.

Analysis: The collected data was analysed by using different statistical technique like Mean, SD and 't' test. The results are given in the following Tables

Table 1: Significant Difference on the Mean Scores of Male and Female Teacher Educators

S.No	Dimension	Gender	Mean	Sd	T Test	Remarks
1.	Total	Male Female	64.3 63.0	0.74 0.92	7.38	S
2.	Ctl	Male Female	60.54 61.62	1.19 1.41	1.48	Ns
3.	Ppt	Male Female	65.04 61.24	3.89 0.98	6.43	S
4.	Int	Male Female	71.07 69.58	1.92 3.35	2.38	S

CTL – Computer in Teaching Learning **PPT** – Power Point Presentation
INT Internet **NS -** Not Significant **S -** Significant

From the above Table it is noted that the 't' values are significantly difference at 5% level of the Teacher Educators for Total, PPT(Power Point Presentation) and INT(Internet) . Total, PPT (Power Point Presentation) and INT (Internet) the Mean score of Male Teacher Educators are higher than the Female Teacher Educators. In CTL(Computer in Teaching Learning) there is no significant difference at 5 % level of the Teacher Educators.

Table 2: Significant Difference on the Mean Scores of Rural and Urban Teacher Educators

S.No	Dimension	Locality	Mean	SD	t test	Remarks
1.	Total	Rural Urban	64.7 63.07	0.837 0.823	5.46	S
2.	CTL	Rural Urban	60.74 63.18	1.61 0.989	1.69	NS
3.	PPT	Rural Urban	62.90 63.07	0.78 0.65	1.06	NS
4.	INT	Rural Urban	74.53 70.93	1.72 1.68	3.62	S

From the above Table, the calculated 't' values are reveal that there is no significant difference at 5% level for the dimensions CTL and PPT. But there exists significant difference at 5% level with respect to Total and INT. In the Total and INT the Mean score of the Rural Teacher Educators are higher having higher awareness on Digital Technology than the Urban Teacher Educators.

Table 3: Significant Difference on the Mean Scores of Science and Arts Teacher Educators

S.No	Dimension	Subject	Mean	SD	t test	Remarks
1.	Total	Science Arts	63.83 64.31	0.929 0.779	1.21	NS
2.	CTL	Science Arts	62.43 61.28	1.06 1.11	4.79	S
3.	PPT	Science Arts	63.02 60.34	4.22 0.934	3.27	S
4.	INT	Science Arts	71.94 73.38	1.19 1.02	6.03	S

The Mean scores and the calculated 't ' values from the above table shows that there is significant difference in all the mean score of CTL, PPT and INT at 5% level except Total. It can be understood that the level Awareness on Digital Technology among Teacher Educators are good in CTL , PPT and INT.

Results and Discussion

The salient findings of the study are i) All the Teacher Educators am having good Awareness on Digitaol Technology. ii) The Mean score of Male Teacher Educators are higher than the Female Teacher Educators towards Awareness on Digital Technology with respect to the dimensions such as Total, PPT and INT. iii) With regards to Locality, the Mean score of Rural Teacher Educators are higher than the Urban Teacher Educators towards Awareness on Digital Technology in Total and INT. iv) The Mean scores of Teacher Educators with respect to Science Subject are higher in CTL, PPT and Arts Teacher Educators are higher in INT.

The result shows that Gender, Locality and Subject of Teacher Educators were not the influencing factor in determining Awareness on Digital Technology. While considering the Gender, Male Teachers are having higher Awareness on Digital Technology than the Female Teachers. This is because Male Teacher Educators may have more time to work in the Computer but the Female Teachers have the commitment to look after their family. By this way Rural Teachers are having Good Awareness on Digital Technology than the Urban Teachers. This is due to the fact that Rural Teachers may show more interest to know about the new things. As well as Science Group Teacher Educators are show more awareness than Art Group Teacher Educators. It may be due to their subject knowledge.

Recommendations for Policy Makings

The result of this study shows that the Teacher Educators are having Good awareness on Digital Technology. Hence the usage of Computer must be increased to develop their practical knowledge. They are having more involvement in using

Digital Technology in their class room Teaching. Effective teaching to promote better learning, proper orientation training Programme must be provided them to develop their knowledge in Digital Technology. The Government must ensure proper training to Teacher Educators to maintain Computers and Electronic things. Educational Authorities should create, improve and sustain the Awareness of Teacher Educators about Computer Knowledge. Teacher Educators should be encouraged by Administrators to use the stand alone Computer Applications in their Teachings. Using Internet application should be given special concentration, because, it empowers and enhance creativity. Digital Technology acts as a catalyst to support change in Teacher Pedagogy.

Conclusion

The Good Awareness on Computer Technology among Primary and Middle School Teachers will show the Conducing Climate towards Educational Technology. The Instruction through Computer has been making wonders in the Class Room Activities. Hence Teachers must have Awareness on Computer Technology to get success and enjoy their Professions.

Reference

1. Best,J.W,(2003). *Research in Education,* Prentice – Hall of India (P) Ltd., New Delhi.
2. Lokesh Koul.(2005). *Methodology of Educational Research*, Vikas Publishing House (P) Ltd, New Delhi.
3. Singh.Y.K,(2005). *Instructional Technology In Education,* P. P. H Publishing
4. Corporation, New Delhi-110002.
5. Sareen.N, (2005). *Information and Communication Technology*, Anmol Publication Pvt.Ltd, New Delhi-110002.

❐

22.

Effectiveness of Multimedia Programme in Perceiving Human Anatomy among Higher Secondary Students

INTRODUCTION

Research work is being continuously done in the field of science and also in the related teaching methods and materials. In order to keep pace with the development of science, the need for new instructional strategies was greatly felt. One such innovative teaching strategy, called multimedia programme, has been chosen and studied by the investigator in this research work. Upgrading Biology curriculum by introducing Human anatomy demands a change in the instructional strategy. The need for developing an instructional strategy for teaching Human anatomy and physiology is very important to make the teachers and students aware of the scientific principles that govern the advances being made in medicine. The functions of the internal organs of human body can be easily explained through a multimedia programme. This also saves the use of expensive chemicals and sophisticated instruments which are beyond the reach of higher secondary schools. In schools, the required equipment to explain the human anatomy is not available. In this situation, the working mechanism of internal organs can be explained by a multimedia programme, which when used as an instructional strategy will make the task of learning human anatomy easier, effective and less expensive. The present study aims to find out the effectiveness of multimedia programme in perceiving human anatomy among higher secondary students in Tindivanam. A samples of 100 higher secondary students selected randomly were studied. A questionnaire method of survey was used to find out the effectiveness of multimedia programme in perceiving human anatomy. The data were collected by using questionnaire as an instrument. Primary data were collected by conducting direct structured interview using questionnaire. All the respondents were asked the same questions in the same fashion and they were informed the purpose of study. Mean, SD, and t-test analysis was applied to test the hypotheses. The findings and observations are the result and outcome of the interpretations made during the study of analysis. The result found that majority of the higher secondary students satisfied about multimedia programme.

In view of growing importance of science education, old concepts of science teaching have therefore, rather become completely outmoded and an entirely new ethos and approach to science curriculum have come into existence. Moreover, unprecedented development of scientific research, new discoveries, and new methods of investigation, in the early twentieth century, has created a need and urge to examine and reorganize science teaching programmes at all levels in schools. Institutions are functioning in an era of rapidly emerging new technologies. Some of them, like information and communications technology, have fuelled a veritable explosion of rising expectations everywhere. When such is the pace of developmental processes, it becomes fairly imperative on the part of the students not only to possess sound knowledge and understanding of fundamental concepts, but also to understand and appreciate the ramifications of various developments in the field of science and technology, especially in the context of their future career. The situation underscores the significance of research in science education and it is time for the educationists to evolve a proper and appropriate strategy for teaching science.

At the Higher Secondary level, the science subject is divided into Physics, Chemistry, Botany, and Zoology according to Tamil Nadu State Board syllabus. Zoology deals with the life history, distribution, structure, reproduction, and importance of animals including Homosapiens, the human beings. 'Human anatomy' is one of the units of the Zoology subject. Human anatomy is the branch of anatomy devoted to the structure of the human body. In general the study of human anatomy helps the students to do their higher studies in Medicine, Physiotherapy, Nursing, Degree courses like B.Sc., Zoology, and Microbiology etc. Apart from acquiring the technical knowledge, it is necessary for human beings to know and control their own systems of their body for healthy life. Hence the investigator has selected the unit "human anatomy" to teach through multimedia programme for the higher secondary students in the present investigation.

An instructional or teaching strategy refers to a pattern of teaching act that serves to attain certain goals and to guard against others. An instructional strategy is a purposefully-conceived and determined plan of action. It also occupies a central position in formal education. Instructional strategies aim at establishing relationship between teaching inputs and learning outputs, mainly in terms of realizing the learning outcomes. Instructional strategies include teaching methods, approaches and techniques.

Methods of instruction may be teacher-centered such as Historical method, Biographical method, Lecture method, Lecture-demonstration method or pupil-centered method which includes group methods such as project method, discussion, seminar and workshop. The pupil-centered methods also include individual methods such as programmed instruction, Computer Aided Instruction, Instructional Modules and Multimedia packages.

REVIEW OF LITERATURE

Chang, Kuo-En et al. (2008) studied **the effects of learning support in simulation-based physics learning.** The results of the study revealed that the outcome for learning about the basic characteristics of an optical lens was significantly better for simulation-based learning than for laboratory learning.

Djeassilane (2008) investigated the effect of computer aided instruction (CAI) in enhancing the academic achievement of higher secondary students in commerce. The findings of the study showed that the computer aided instruction was effective in helping the students of the experimental group to perform better in the post-test. It proved the effectiveness of the computer aided instruction in commerce developed by the investigator. And also it was found that the experimental students had more favourable attitude towards computer assisted instruction.

Garnett, Hackling and Oliver (2009) developed an interactive multimedia package to improve students' understanding of the particulate basis of chemical reaction, and their ability to interpret chemical equations and solve problems based on equations. The study showed that Interactive multimedia provided learners with access to a rich information source and appropriate activities to promote learning and understanding.

Junaidu, Sahalu (2009) studied effectiveness of multimedia in learning & teaching data structures online. This paper explores and reports on the importance of creating multimedia-rich course content and the important role that animations can play in creating a successful online learning experience. Results indicated that students consistently perform much better in questions requiring application of material taught in carefully animated algorithms. These results should carry over to other educational environments.

Liao, Yuen-kuang C., Chang, Huei-wen and Chen, Yu-wen (2009) compared the effects of computer applications (i.e., computer-assisted instruction, computer simulations, and Web-based learning) versus traditional instruction on elementary school students' achievement in Taiwan. The results suggest that computer application instruction is more effective than traditional instruction for elementary school students in Taiwan.

O'Day, Danton (2010) studied on "using animations to teach biology: past & future research on the attributes that underlie pedagogically sound animations".

Multiple technical resources (commonly referred to as multimedia) are currently used by many instructors to communicate difficult topics and concepts to their students in meaningful ways. Various sources have shown that animations are more effective than static sequential images. This study evaluated how animations can be and have been used as effective teaching and learning tools in biology and what more needs to be done to understand their true value.

Ozmen, Haluk (2010) studied on "The influence of CAI on students' conceptual understanding of chemical Bonding and attitude towards chemistry: A case for Turkey". The results of this study suggested that teaching-learning of topics in chemistry related to chemical bonding can be improved by the use of computer-assisted teaching materials.

Ponraj and Nellaiyapen (2010) investigated the effectiveness of CAI in teaching Zoology. The major finding of the study showed that the experimental group performed better than the Control group in the post-test. The results of the study revealed that experimental method of teaching is more effective than the traditional method of teaching the topic 'Nucleus' in Zoology.

Pryor, Caroline and Bitter, Gary (2010) used multimedia to teach in-service teachers and studied its impacts on learning, application, and retention. The study found that the video modeling in the module was effective in helping teachers learn, and discourse strategies were learned, applied, and retained.

Rotbain, Marbach-Ad and Stavy (2011) used a computer animation to teach high school molecular biology. The achievements of the experimental group were compared with those of a control group. Analysis of the post-test showed that the mean score of the experimental group was significantly higher than the mean score of the control group.

Venkataraman (2011) prepared software packages (CAI) for XI standard physics and studied the effectiveness of it's among selected modes of CAI in physics in relation to learners' personality. The results of the study showed that the CAI is effective with different modes. Computer Assisted Instruction shows significant difference in the achievement of different instructional objectives. Further Computer Assisted Instruction enhances the retention of the learnt content.

Vernadakis et al. (2012) examined the effect of multimedia computer-assisted instruction (MCAI), traditional instruction (TI), and combined instruction (CI) methods on learning the skill of shooting in basketball. Additionally, a comparison of the students' attitudes towards the MCAI and TI methods was made. Students took pre-, post-, and retention written test covering techniques and rules of the games. Post-test results indicated no significant differences between the groups concerning the written test. Nevertheless, the attitude test scores of the CI group were more favourable to MCAI method than the TI method. Retention test results showed that groups retained the knowledge acquisition. However, the combined method of instruction tended to be the most effective for cognitive learning.

Victor, Adeosun Olufemi (2012) investigated the relative effects of three multi-media instructional packages on Nigerian students' achievement in social studies. The purpose was to determine which of the combinations of videotape recording presentation, pictures and the chalk and talk method; the combination of audiotape recording presentation, pictures and the chalk and talk method and the combination of pictures and the chalk and talk method. The study revealed that the combination of pictures and the chalk and talk method was most effective among the packages tested in the learning of social studies.

OBJECTIVES

1. To develop a Multimedia Programme for the unit of Human anatomy from XI standard Zoology subject in order to teach the higher secondary students.
2. To find out the effectiveness of Multimedia Programme in teaching Human anatomy among higher secondary students.

METHODOLOGY

The methodology adopted for the study is explained in detail. The sampling technique, size of the sample, variables of the study, description of the tool used and administration of tool are elaborated.

Sample

A samples of 100 higher secondary students in selected randomly were studied in Tindivanam Town.

Data Collection

The present study aims at developing and using Multimedia programme for perceiving human anatomy for higher secondary students to enable them to understand the concepts very easily through individualized instructional technique. It is maintained that the Multimedia programme may reduce monotony in the classroom by bringing out real life situations and motivate them for self-study and provides opportunities for individual pace and ability.

The study intends to develop a multimedia programme for human anatomy for XI standard Zoology subject prescribed by Tamil Nadu State Board Syllabus and find out the effectiveness of the Multimedia programme through experimentation in perceiving human anatomy among the higher secondary students. The study provides scope for the development and use of many Multimedia programmes in the concerned discipline as well as other disciplines for the benefit of learners of different categories. Hence the multimedia programme can be used as an individualized instructional technique for the students of different categories in the science subjects as well as other subjects.

ANALYSIS AND INTERPRETATION

Performance of control group students between the pre test and post test in human anatomy.

The Mean, Standard Deviation and Co-efficient of Variation were computed for the control group students in their performance in human anatomy between the pre test and post test.

Table 1: Distribution of Mean, Standard Deviation and Co-efficient of Variation on the performance of control group students between the pre test and post test in human anatomy

Group	N	Mean	S.D	CV
Pre test	100	42.69	13.60	31.86
Post test	100	52.46	13.28	25.31

The Co-efficient of Variation of the pre test and post test for the control group students was found to be 31.86 and 25.31, which reveals that the control group students are more consistent in their performance in human anatomy in the post test than the pre test. It reveals that the control group students have improved in their performance in human anatomy in the post test than the pre test.

To find out the significance of the difference between the control and experimental group students in their performance in human anatomy in the pre test, the 't' test was used.

Table 2:Distribution of 't' value between the control and experimental group students in their performance in human anatomy in the pre test

Group	N	Mean	S.D	't' value	Level of Significant
Control	100	42.69	13.60	0.17	p>0.05
Experimental	100	43.31	12.59		

There is no significant difference between the control and experimental group students in their performance in human anatomy in the pre test.

The obtained 't' value 0.17 is not statistically significant since it is less than the table 't' value 1.96 for 50 df at 0.05 level of significance. Hence the null hypothesis is accepted. It shows that there is no significant difference between the control and experimental group students in their performance in human anatomy in the pre test. It is therefore concluded that both control and experimental group students have the same level of performance in human anatomy in the pre test.

To find out the significance of the difference between the control and experimental group students in their performance in human anatomy in the post test, the 't' test was used.

Table 3:Distribution of 't' value between the control and experimental group students in their performance in human anatomy in the post test

Group	N	Mean	S.D	't' value	Level of Significant
Control	100	52.46	13.28	14.38	p<0.05
Experimental	100	92.81	5.31		

There is no significant difference between the control and experimental group students in their performance in human anatomy in the post test.

The obtained 't' value 14.38 is statistically significant since it is greater than the table 't' value 1.96 for 50 df at 0.05 level of significance. Hence the null hypothesis is rejected. It shows that there is significant difference between the control and experimental group students in their performance in human anatomy in the post test. It is therefore concluded that the experimental group students performed significantly better in human anatomy than that of control group students in the post test.

To find out the significance of the difference between the pre and post test mean scores of control group students in the performance in human anatomy, the 't' was used.

Table 4: Distribution of 't' value for the pre and post test mean scores of control group students in the performance in human anatomy

Group	N	Mean	S.D	't' value	Level of Significant
Pre test	100	42.69	13.60	2.62	p<0.05
Post test	100	52.46	13.28		

There is no significant difference between the pre and post test mean scores of control group students in the performance in human anatomy.

The obtained 't' value 2.62 is statistically significant since it is greater than the table 't' value 1.96 for 50 df at 0.05 level of significance. Hence the null hypothesis is rejected. It shows that there is significant difference between the pre and post test mean scores of control group students in the performance in human anatomy. It is therefore concluded that the control group students have improved in their performance in human anatomy in the post test.

SUGGESTIONS

The present study aims at developing and using Multimedia programme for perceiving human anatomy for higher secondary students to enable them to understand the concepts very easily through individualized instructional technique. It is maintained that the Multimedia programme may reduce monotony in the classroom by bringing out real life situations and motivate them for self-study and provides opportunities for individual pace and ability.

CONCLUSION

The study intends to develop a multimedia programme for human anatomy for XI standard Zoology subject prescribed by Tamil Nadu State Board Syllabus and find out the effectiveness of the Multimedia programme through experimentation in perceiving human anatomy among the higher secondary students. The study provides scope for the development and use of many Multimedia programmes in the concerned discipline as well as other disciplines for the benefit of learners of different categories. Hence the multimedia programme can be used as an individualized instructional technique for the students of different categories in the science subjects as well as other subjects.

The present study reveals that the experiment group students who used multimedia programme performed significantly better than that of the control group students who did not use, which implies that the multimedia programme has tremendous impact upon the performance in human anatomy than the students learning through traditional method. This proves the effectiveness of the multimedia programme in human anatomy developed by the investigator.

The present study reveals that the performance of the control and experimental group students in the post test is significantly higher than the pre test. But the performance of the experimental group students in the post test is more significantly higher than the post test performance of control group students. Thus, it proves the supremacy of the multimedia programme over traditional method.

REFERENCES

1. Chang, Kuo-En; Chen, Yu-Lung; Lin, He-Yan; Sung, Yao-Ting (2008). Effects of learning support in simulation-based physics learning. Computers & Education, 51(4): 1486-1498..
2. Djeassilane, N. (2008). Effect of computer aided instruction (CAI) in enhancing the academic achievement of higher secondary students in commerce. Unpublished Doctoral Dissertation, Alagappa University, Karaikudi.
3. Garnett, P., Hackling, M., & Oliver, R. (2009). Designing interactive multimedia materials to support concept development in beginning chemistry classes.
4. Junaidu, Sahalu (2009). Effectiveness of multimedia in learning & teaching data structures online. Turkish Online Journal of Distance Education-TOJDE, 9(4), Article 7. Retrieved March.
5. Liao, Yuen-kuang C., Chang, Huei-wen & Chen, Yu-wen (2009). Effects of Computer Applications on Elementary School Students' Achievement: A Meta-Analysis of Students in Taiwan. Computers in the Schools, 24(3-4): 43-64. Retrieved.
6. O'Day, Danton H. (2010). Using animations to teach biology: past & future research on the attributes that underlie pedagogically sound animations.

The American Biology Teacher, 70(5):274-278. Retrieved March 20.

7. Ozmen, Haluk (2010). The influence of Computer-Assisted Instruction on students' conceptual understanding of chemical Bonding and Attitude toward chemistry: A case for Turkey. Computers and Education, 51(1): 423-438. Retrieved March.
8. Ponraj, P., & Nellaiyapen, N. O. (2010). CAI in teaching Zoology. Research and Reflections on Education, 6(2): 18-21.
9. Pryor, Caroline R., & Bitter, Gary G. (2010). Using multimedia to teach in-service teachers: Impacts on learning, application, and retention. Computers in Human Behavior, 24 (6): 2668-2681. Retrieved March.
10. Rotbain, Y., Marbach-Ad, G., & Stavy, R. (2011). Using a computer animation to teach high school molecular biology. Journal of Science Education and Technology, 17(1): 49-58. Retrieved March.
11. Venkataraman, S. (2011). Relative effectiveness among selected modes of CAI in physics in relation to learner's personality. Unpublished Doctoral Dissertation, Annamalai University. Chidambaram.
12. Vernadakis, N., Zetou, E., Tsitskari, E., Giannousi, M., & Kioumourtzoglou, E. (2012). Student attitude and learning outcomes of multimedia computer-assisted versus traditional instruction in basketball. Education and Information Technologies, 13(3): 167-183.
13. Victor, Adeosun Olufemi (2012). Relative effects of three Multi-Media Instructional Packages on Nigerian student's achievement in Social Studies. Pakistan Journal of Social Sciences, 5 (5): 415 – 420. Retrieved March.

❑❑❑